I'll Never Be Fat Again!

I'll Never Be Fat Again!

Carole Livingston Stuart

New York•New York
www.barricadebooks.com

Published by Barricade Books Inc.
150 Fifth Avenue
Suite 700
New York, NY 10011

Library of Congress Cataloging-in-Publication Data
Livingston-Stuart, Carole.
    I'll never be fat again/Carole Livingston Stuart—2nd trade
        pbk. ed., rev., updated, and expanded.
    p. cm.
    Includes bibliographical references.
    ISBN: 1-56980-148-7
    1. Reducing—Psychological aspects. 2. Reducing. I. Title.
RM222.2.L537 2000
613.2'5—dc20
                                              91-40267
                                                   CIP

Printed in the United States of America.

10 9 8 7 6 5 4 3 2 1

Contents

For L.
Without you there would be
nothing. You make it all
happen.

Also by Carole Livingston
How To Lose Five Pounds Fast
To Turn You On
Why Was I Adopted?
Why Am I Going to the Hospital? (with Claire Ciliotta)

Preface

From time to time, people have commented with surprise on how thin I am, while at the same time I seem to be eating everything in sight. I am and have been a member of a number of gourmet societies. I belong to the Wine & Food Society, an international gourmet organization. I once belonged to the *Confrerie de la Chaine des Rotisseurs* as well as *Les Amis du Vin*. Only time constraints have caused me to drop out of these groups although I occasionally still attend events with friends who are members. I read restaurant reviews all the time and clip those that look promising, making a mental note to try out the latest "hot" chef.

In Paris, I dine at three-star restaurants such as Lassere (I'm a member of their Casserole Club) and Le Taillevent.

I own at least fifty cookbooks and read about food and cooking all the time. One of my favorite things to watch on television is the Cooking Channel.

Many of my friends are foodies, too. This means feasts at their homes, and feasts at mine.

Recently, I supervised an exotic dinner comprising twenty-five different delicacies for a group of more than one hundred guests.

I was co-host of an ice-cream tasting! The most highly-praised ice creams from all over America were flown into New York so that members of the Wine & Food

Society could sample twelve scrumptious flavors, ranging from Graeter's chocolate chip from Cincinnati, to butter almond from Bischoff's of Teaneck, New Jersey.

I love food. But I love being thin too.
I'm five feet, four inches tall.
This morning I weighed myself.
I weigh 122 pounds.
I once weighed 162.
I'm not now the thinnest woman alive—nor was I the fattest.

But I'm thin and I like myself and I'll never be fat again.
Interested?

Introduction

What You Will Find in this Book—and What You Won't

Would you like to know how I did it? If you're an overweight person or even a person "on the brink" then I'm going to help you *if you want to help yourself.*

You've heard that song before. The reducing business is a huge one. There are whole industries that produce diets, diet books, diet pills, diet candies, diet supplements, and diet gadgets.

Not many women's or health and fitness magazines would dare publish two consecutive issues without offering something in the way of weight-reducing advice. We're bombarded with dieting information all the time. Lack of information is not the problem. The problem is that few of us understand ourselves, and most of us don't understand our involvement with food.

The key to it all is so simple that it just *seems* profound.

Recently, at lunch, I said something in passing to the editor of a national magazine. I hadn't meant to say anything momentous, but later she told me it changed her life.

The topic of conversation was my history as a thin person after years of being a fat one.

I mentioned to her that at a certain point in my life I realized that in order to be slender I would have to give

3

up something. I would have to overcome my childish instinct for instant gratification in order to obtain the greater gratification inherent in my becoming thin. Unbeknownst to me, this comment started her on a serious program of weight reduction.

A happy ending to the editor's story is that upon losing weight, she found her Prince Charming. But I don't want you to believe that the reward for being thin is romance. Rather, being thin produces its own satisfaction. You will like yourself thin. If someone else happens to like you, too—great!—that's a bonus.

If you have a weight problem, deep in your heart-of-hearts you've known the following for a long time: being overweight is dangerous to your health. Extra pounds precipitate certain illnesses and increase the propensity for others. Excess pounds shorten your life span.

But you've known this before I wrote it, and it hasn't stopped you from remaining fat, anymore than the knowledge of the damage caused by cigarette smoking have convinced millions to discontinue that slow-suicide habit.

The pleasure instinct is a strong one, so strong that we have a social word for an excess of it: hedonism. Sometimes the pleasure urge is so powerful that it leads people to such self-destructive acts as inhaling "angel dust" and cocaine, injecting heroin, or abusing the body with other dangerous drugs.

People have literally eaten themselves to death. I read about a woman who, while being carried by stretcher to a waiting ambulance, confessed that she had overdosed on Mounds candy bars!

An extreme case? Perhaps. But every overweight person has experienced overeating to the point of illness.

If you think the above example extreme, how about the man who weighed 1,400 pounds. *1,400 pounds!* He went on a fast, but his body retained all fluids. He wasn't eliminating any waste. He was killing himself by dieting! The fire department's rescue squad had to remove a window from his house to get him out. They fashioned a stretcher out of thick plywood to cart him to the hospital. He did lose 900 pounds and was on his way down to normal weight. Unfortunately, at last report, he had died. No amount of effort could save him.

But back to less extreme examples. Like you and me. Body types are familiar to us all. Many books have charts to show you how much you should weigh for your height and frame. Although the scientific formula has changed, they still are dedicated to letting you know you are overweight. I know it intimately. When I was fat I always conveniently fit myself into the "large frame" category. Unfortunately, I never could manage to increase my height to adjust my actual weight to the "proper" one listed on the charts!

You are not going to find any such charts in this book. To paraphrase an old Flip Wilson joke, you overweight people know who you are. Besides, don't we look at these charts trying to convince ourselves that we aren't as fat as we *know* we are?

In these pages, you also will not find recommendations to buy any of those frequently advertised gadgets and scales that tell you how much fat you have on your body.

One such device is a caliper which is used in the "pinch test." The pinch test measures the amount of fat in specific areas on the body, such as the back of the upper arm or a spot just above the hip. I'm not sure what you are supposed to learn after you've pinch-tested yourself. You may have the type of body that does not have a lot of fat in those particular areas. If that's the case and you "pass" the pinch test, does that mean you aren't fat?

A recent letter to the editor of *Health Magazine* asked about the accuracy of such a test. The writer wondered if the test exaggerated her overall percentage since she tended to carry extra weight in her arms and stomach—two of the spots her gym measures.

The editor agreed that caliper tests can be as accurate as fancier methods, but the results, as suggested by the American College of Sports Medicine, should be compiled after measuring at seven sites, including the chest and hips, rather than only three (upper arm, stomach and thigh).

Another item you can buy is a scale that tells your body fat percentage by sending an electrical charge (absolutely painless) up through your heels as you stand on two metal disks. The accuracy is questionable, but many have been sold.

There are even more sophisticated methods of measuring body fat. But face it: these are not targeted to the average person. And certainly not to thin people.

I have never met a thin person who bought one of these gadgets. Anyone who does buy these items is doing it more for reassurance that they aren't really overweight than for practical use. The fact again is, people who buy them know they are fat. We all share a secret wish that one day, one of these gadgets will show us that we aren't fat?

To repeat: thin people don't buy them. As a matter of fact, *many thin people don't even own a scale!* How many overweight people can make that claim?

Jack H. Wilmore, Ph.D., a professor of physical education at the University of Arizona, tells us that at birth we start out with ten to twelve percent body fat. By the time we are in our early twenties, this has increased to fifteen percent for men and twenty-five percent for women. Because we eat too much and exercise too little, we have a tendency to increase *both* our total fat as well as the ratio of fat to the rest of our body weight.

If that's not discouraging enough, Dr. Wilmore points out that on average, Americans gain "one pound of weight a year after twenty-five—which adds up to thirty additional pounds by age fifty-five."

Do you *really* want to figure out your fat percentage? Then go to a sports physiology lab where they will weigh you underwater in a special tank, because fat is lighter than water. You are told your total volume, and guess what, you can look up on a table to find out what your fat percentage is! So, what have you accomplished? You've now traded height/weight charts for fat percentage tables!

One of the most popular forms of cosmetic surgery is liposuction. This is when fat is literally vacuumed out of places on your body, you don't want it. Although the claim is once those fat cells are removed, they never come back again, if you gain weight, the fat does come back. Not in the place from which it's been suctioned, but elsewhere on the body.

Only recently has the danger of liposuction been getting publicity as people seeking a quick fix sucked out a few pounds of fat and discovered that it is not a simple procedure. Indeed, if something goes wrong—and it may—you could end up in serious trouble—possibly life-threatening.

But even if you want to risk the potential danger, you may be trading off slim thighs for fat arms later if you start putting on weight again.

Where does this leave you? Still fat. You won't find any recommendations here about finding out your fat ratio.

What you *will* find in this book is a sound, sensible, workable and realistic approach to getting thin—*and staying thin.*

It's the staying thin that's important. Nay, *critical*! If you're a dieting veteran, you know about the formerly fat lady psychiatrist who became fat again, even as she was touring for a book that described how she'd become thin. And we've all watched Oprah battle to keep her weight down, even employing a full-time trainer and cook.

This book is different. It reveals a successful approach because I have been in your war, fought all the battles, *and I have won!*

Unlike people who write diet books, I'm not going to load you with lists of specific foods to eat or not to eat. I'm not going to tell you when to eat your meals. I am going to share with you some vital concepts I have learned about reducing that will help you. I will share with you the ultimate secrets of becoming thin. *And I will tell you how to stay there.*

First of all, I'm lucky, because the first time I became aware of a need to reduce, I was only thirteen years old. You may wonder, "What's so lucky about that?" After all, many people spend youth and many years beyond that totally unaware of what they put into their mouths. But I have observed that sooner or later—even those people who have been "naturally thin" all their lives begin to put on weight.

Since I became overweight at an early age, I've had a lot more time to learn about reducing. I almost feel sorry for those who suddenly find themselves with more pounds than they'd like to be carrying, and feeling hopeless about where to start. For them it's more difficult. Not impossible—just more difficult.

But now I want to tell you my story.

Important:

Throughout this book, there are chapters to which Intermission Exercises have been appended, and others which have lists to help you. If you really intend to get the most out of this book, please don't just turn pages. Don't pass by the Intermission Exercises or lists. Take the time to do the exercises, and study the lists before going on to the next chapter. It won't take much time and your time will be well-spent because these are designed to be truly helpful.

INTERMISSION

•**Sit still in a quiet place and think about how and when you got heavy, and why you think you stay that way.**

•**Do this for five uninterrupted minutes—by the clock.**

1

My Story

I was the thin one in my family. Thin, that is, only by comparison. My father was 6'3" tall. Tall, but not enough to justify the 240 pounds he usually weighed. My mother was only five-feet tall. Most of the time she weighed in at 185. And my sister, at five-feet-seven inches, frequently carried well over 200 pounds.

With examples like them I didn't stand a chance.

As I said earlier, by the time I was thirteen I was already chubby. Naturally, no one in my home took notice. But at school, where many of my friends were petite and slim, I became self-conscious. "Birds of a feather" frequently do flock together, and so I gravitated towards the other chubby girls with whom I could guiltlessly share the delights of the yummy chocolate iced cupcakes which happened to be a specialty at our school cafeteria.

A few years later, in high school, my main ambition was to become a cheerleader. By then I had accumulated more than just a few extra pounds. And thus came the first time when I had to face a dilemma I would encounter many more times in the future. I wanted to be a cheerleader. I also wanted to keep eating those cupcakes. I wasn't stupid; I knew I couldn't have my cupcakes and eat them, too.

I had to give up something in order to obtain something else. And the something else was *very* important to me at that point in my life.

I want to repeat this because it is such a critical point: *I had to give up something in order to attain something more important to me.*

I didn't give it up right away. It seemed that no sooner had I conquered my chocolate-iced-cupcake craving, than something equally tempting came into view. Along with struggling to overcome the need to find someone who had the same problem. (Remember those same feathered birds?)

In this instance both the temptation and technique were in one package. While many of my friends were slim and petite, Phyllis was not. She and I clung to each other like hot fudge clings to cold ice cream.

Phyllis and I spent a lot of time complaining to each other about being overweight. Much of the rest of our time was taken up feeding ourselves from the never-ending variety of freshly baked cookies that Phyllis' mother made in (I swear) ten pound batches. When these ran low, we would slip into the dining room where six different kinds of candy were always available. These were piled high on a lazy Susan server which, when rotated, temptingly displayed the selections.

My favorite was, and still is, milk chocolate bark. If you don't know what chocolate bark is, you are missing a taste treat. Simply described, it is chocolate candy with nuts throughout (my favorite was almond) that is broken from a large "sheet" by the vendor. Not any of that fancy boxed stuff; this is candy for the hard-core aficionado.

Let us pause for a moment. Consider the above paragraph and note how vividly I remember that chocolate bark. I was barely an adolescent when I first tasted it; it's years since I last tasted it, yet the taste memory clings to me vividly.

I believed when I was trying to reduce, that once you got thin—*Vogue* thin—you never wanted those things that made you fat in the first place. Total victory would be mine, I thought, and I would never gaze longingly at a cream puff or a Malomar cookie again.

Well, let me tell you a truth. There are some foods that no longer have the same importance to me. I can, and quite comfortably do, live without them.

I know people who are really crazy about cheese. Cheese and I parted company when I discovered the Pritikin Program which virtually eliminates all but non-fat or low-fat cheeses, and milk products from your diet. Brie? I barely remember the last time I had any. Of course, take me to Paris where cheese is not just cheese, but rather a taste treat not to be missed, and I eat cheese.

What I'm saying about other foods that I love—that add pounds—is that I still crave them. I can still conjure up not only their images, but their taste as well. And, should I ever be locked in a room by myself and someone slips a dish of chocolate bark under the door, you can bet that dish will be empty in a matter of minutes.

Temptation is *always* there. Those foods will always call to us. And sometimes we eat them.

What then is the difference in our behavior? Well, remember in the beginning of this chapter I said I discovered that in order to attain something important I would have to give up something else? (In this case, the chocolate bark candy.)

The difference is not that I don't eat it. I do. The difference is that now I don't eat it most of the time.

I have a built-in scale in my body. This scale doesn't measure weight. It measures desire. It talks to me and I talk back. We have conversations all the time. Most of the time the dialogue goes something like this:

Me: "Wow! That lemon meringue pie looks delicious."

Scale: "Careful! You know what lemon meringue pie can do to your waistline, not to mention your cholesterol level."

Me: "Yes, but look at it! That meringue must be six inches high!"

Scale: "When was the last time you ate lemon meringue pie?"

Me: "About six years ago"

Scale: "How was it?"

Me: "Well ... not so terrific. As a matter of fact, the crust turned out to be soggy. And the meringue only looked fluffy. It tasted like soap bubbles. I think I got sick."

Scale: "Well, think it over."

Okay, I've exaggerated to make a point. In reality, however, I do *consciously* gauge how much I want a "forbidden" food against how much I'll have to pay for it. Payment, of course in pounds, not dollars. Much of the time I decide it just isn't worth the price. Sometimes I decide it is. *And then I eat it.* And I eat it without any guilt at all. Because I have made the decision. *The food hasn't decided for me* .

This brings me to a word that I want to reclaim.

"Forbidden." When we reach the point of making conscious decisions about what we eat, there aren't any forbidden foods.

Dr. Nevin Scrimshaw, head of Nutrition and Food Science at Massachusetts Institute of Technology, concurs. He points out that "There is no such thing as a 'fattening' food—any food eaten to caloric excess (when we consume more calories than we expend as energy) will make us gain weight."

You may substitute my word "forbidden" for Dr. Scrimshaw's "fattening". Keeping those two words in mind, remember too that the foods we select and the way we prepare them has a lot to do with the number of calories and grams of fat, salt and cholesterol we consume. Rather than banishing the food from our diet, we must learn to forbid ourselves the preparation of these foods in ways that will put more pounds on our bodies and clog our arteries.

For instance—what about potatoes? Ahh! Remember potatoes? Most dieters avoid them like botulism. They are fattening, right? Wrong! The fact is, potatoes are fairly low in calories and are a pretty good source of vitamin C. But, if you slice them and fry them in oil, they become French fries; when you mash them with butter and milk, they become mashed potatoes. Get the message? Obviously, it is what we add to the potato that makes the calorie count shoot up. Potatoes in and of themselves have an undeservedly bad reputation.

The baked potato has become a mainstay of my diet. I often eat one with a salad for my lunch or dinner. I don't top it with sour cream, but rather with a variety of low-calorie, fat-free toppings like salsa or mustard or steamed mushrooms and onions, etc.

Another "forbidden" food to most dieters used to be pasta. Would it surprise you to discover that you can eat more pasta than French fried potatoes for fewer calories and have a good protein source at the same time?

All dieters could benefit from a quickie course in food values and nutrition. Our ideas would change about what is "forbidden" and what isn't. Again: *It's what we do to food and how much of it we eat that adds the fat, not the food itself.*

I want to say something more about what we can now refer to as non-forbidden foods and about conscious decisions.

If I could relive those days I spent with Phyllis and the cookies and the lazy Susan bearing candy, and put my current attitudes into action here's what would happen:

I'd look at the cookies and the candy and think about them. I would try (though not always successfully) not to eat them without being aware of the pleasure that I wanted to derive from the experience. After all, what's the point of eating only to nourish a guilty conscience? I would thoroughly enjoy a selection of cookies—making sure I had at least one of each kind.

I would then turn to the candy and very possibly eat more than I intended of the chocolate bark. But this time I would definitely skip the gumdrops and spice drops. I've discovered that I don't really love them all that much. And I hate the way they cling to my teeth, making work and money for my dentist.

Do you get the point?

The important difference in my eating pattern today is that I now eat by selection. Selection is when you make the decision that you really do in fact want a specific food. You have thought about it for a while. (This can be seconds, minutes, hours, even days) and you have concluded that eating it is worthwhile; even though it may mean skipping something else.

Here's an example of what I do. Not long ago I located a bakery that makes one thing better than any other bakery I have ever found: giant chocolate chip cookies. (In case you haven't figured it out by now, I am a great fan of things chocolate!) I really love these cookies. It takes quite a bit of effort for me to get to this bakery since it is not near my home. So... when I decide that I have to have a chocolate chip cookie, I think about it and plan for it. And when I get it—I consume it with total pleasure.

There is almost a ritual attached to it. Since I know I am going to eat it and want to enjoy it thoroughly, I make sure to pick a time when I can accomplish that. It's usually around 9:00 p.m. when I'm ready for my evening mug of tea. I used to do this after my daughter, Jenni, was asleep so I didn't have to share any of my cookie. This is not a sharing moment. It's a time I reserve for my own personal indulgence. Now Jenni is married and can get her own cookies. But I still go through the whole exercise just the same. And I don't share my cookie with my husband, either. Well, maybe just a few crumbs with Tara, my toy poodle.

Selfish?

Sure. But I believe we are all entitled to some things in life that don't have to be shared with others.

When you get to the point of planning to have some favorite item, go ahead. Enjoy it.

When I make this decision I never feel guilty about eating. When I eat without thought, I suffer acutely. Because for me, guilt usually drives me further into unconscious eating. And that's a tough cycle to break.

Tough, but not impossible. The noted psychologist, Dr. Albert Ellis, points out that *now* is the time to break the cycle. Not at the end of the day or week or month. The moment you find yourself bingeing is the time to get control. Whoever set the arbitrary rule that Monday or the first of the month or New Year's Day or the first of July was the time to begin diets? Any minute of any hour of any day is the time to stop bingeing. And don't waste time berating yourself for having fallen off the wagon. Just get back on! I guarantee you that you'll feel good about yourself for having stopped the binge.

2

My Family

Mentally draw your family's physical (health) profile. Are You the exception, or are other members of your family also overweight?
Have any of them ever reduced—and stayed thin?

As mentioned before, my entire family was fat. And not just by a few pounds. I mean *really* fat. My sister, Jane, who was two years my elder, was always seriously overweight. Even as a child I remember seeing how she suffered the taunts and teasing of children her own age because of her size.

One day I asked my mother when Jane first became fat. She told me it was after she'd had her appendix removed. Hearing that explanation, I thereafter associated appendectomies with getting heavy. Not until many years later did I discover that Jane had her appendix removed when she was five years old! I suppose my family wanted to believe it was the operation that caused her to gain weight. It probably made them feel less guilty about her being heavy at a time in her life when she had little responsibility for it.

I am intense about the subject of children and weight. Watching Jane spend a tortured childhood (that is not an exaggeration because children can be cruel to each other when they find even the smallest flaw) is perhaps one of my most vivid memories. As a girl, Jane could only shop in the "chubbies" department. Later it was into half sizes. When she did manage to lose some weight, she could never keep it off.

My parents don't deserve all the blame. As an adult, it was Jane who kept herself fat. However, my folks obviously didn't teach either of us proper eating habits. In that way they certainly helped keep her heavy, and started me on the road to having a weight problem.

When Jane and I were children, chubby babies were considered cute. This is a concept that exists in some other countries to this day. In Greece, a person who has an enormous belly signifies someone who has a lot to eat—and thus a person to be admired. There the average weight—especially of women and children—is between 12 and 16 pounds heavier than the European and American average. Fatness and appetite are associated with good health.

This distorted idea arose in Greece as the result of many years of food shortages. For example, during World War II several hundred thousand Greeks died of starvation. It's no surprise that heavy eating became associated with life and with health. Now, however, the Greek nation is campaigning to make people aware that obesity is a negative goal.

Awareness of the dangers of obesity has increased. Medical researchers have concluded that the number of fat cells we have is determined at childhood. Once you have more fat cells than normal, the best you can hope to do is to keep them at a normal size. Unfortunately, people with more fat cells than normal will always have more difficulty reducing.

Parents have a responsibility to educate their children about the benefits of good eating habits. If they do a good job, their kids may never need a diet book.

How can parents prevent children from becoming obese? For one thing, they can stop interpreting feeding as a demonstration of love. In some cultures, food is so entwined with the concept of giving and receiving love that to refuse to eat is interpreted as an outright rejection of the person offering the food.

Parents can stop using food as a reward or a pacifier. Dr. Hilde Bruch, a psychiatrist at the Baylor University School of Medicine in Houston, Texas, says, "All the mother has to do is give the child food whenever he cries, no matter what the reason for the distress, or not feed him when he's hungry because it's not yet time to eat again."

What then happens is that the child will have no will power. His brain will never learn to distinguish hunger from being bored, feeling depressed or disappointed. And he will have one reaction to all of these feelings: he will eat.

Instead, feed children when they are hungry rather than on a specific schedule—and don't make them eat if they are not hungry.

I was determined that my daughter not have a weight problem, at least not of my doing. I had to unlearn many of the habits I learned as a child in order to help Jenni grow up unselfconscious about her eating. I made a determined effort to not urge her to "Eat," and instead, I watched her appetite patterns. The fact is, she has a very small appetite. Instead of filling her plate with food that she would leave (and aggravate me), I gave her tiny portions. If she wanted more, she asked for it. If she didn't, I accepted her decision that she'd had enough.

The result: Jenni grew up without a weight problem. She became one of those "naturally thin" people I envied as a child. She has a good appetite, sometimes overeats, and even puts on a few pounds now and then. However, the difference is, no matter how much she enjoys what she is eating she stops when she's had enough. She doesn't do this consciously; she just does it naturally.

I'm proud of the part I have played in letting Jenni

grow up without focusing on food as reward/punishment. And equally important, she grew up without having a food disorder, which so many of our young people suffer.

Observe your children. As infants they instinctively stop eating when they are full. But even at five and six years old they start to take on the habits we have taught them—and overeat. If you make your children believe that cleaning their plates makes you happy, why, that's just what they'll do. They'll try to please you, and that's not the purpose of eating.

It's difficult to look at a baby in a crib and realize that you are presenting that child with a serious emotional problem by overfeeding it. As that infant grows into a chubby toddler, a stout youngster, and a chunky teenager, he or she will require a thick suit of emotional armor for self-protection.

The child may act happy because that's one way to defend against hurtful comments, ridicule and feeling bad about one's image.

Contrary to that age-old notion, fat people are not jolly. Oh, they may act jolly, but as Jane used to confess, "What else can I do? Should I cry when people make fun of me?"

Rather than cry, many fat people pretend they don't care about the ribbing they take. And they usually do a convincing job. That's because fat people are treated as if they were a separate race.

Even alcoholics often evoke more sympathy than fat people. Being fat is an undeniable admission that you can't control yourself. And, to most of the world, overeating shows a childish lack of self-control.

Losing control by overeating isn't any worse than losing control by drinking too much. But socially it creates a great deal of prejudice against the obese person. The alcoholic can hide his problem for a while, but let's face it, fat people stand out because their problem shows.

Sure, it's unfair, but that's the way things are.

There have been attempts to organize fat people to convince themselves and others that they are content being fat. Let them come up with all the zippy slogans they want, I will never be convinced that fat people are happy about their size.

I do believe that fat people suffer mightily.

If there's a case for being fat, I won't present it. This is a book to help you lose weight—not to make you feel great about being heavy. However, having watched Jane grow up very heavy and suffer because of it, I am sympathetic to the emotional plight of obese people.

Once in awhile Jane managed to slim down for a short period. She was very pretty. I know what you are thinking... but Jane *was* pretty.

Unfortunately, there was not enough motivation going for her to stay thin. And inevitably, the pounds would creep back onto her. Later, as a young adult she married a rather thin fellow. If it was not tragic, it would have been comical because of the obvious Jack Sprat comparison. Jane's husband liked her being fat. Well, it's not that he liked her fat, but as I have discovered about many relationships, as long as she stayed fat, he felt less threatened about losing her affection. Whenever she tried to reduce, he worried that she would become attractive to other men, and then he'd risk losing her.

I'm sure you've encountered situations like that. In such cases, you've got the thin one mouthing weight-reduction encouragement, even while subtly sabotaging the reducing program.

"Aw, go on, honey, it won't hurt just this once to have a piece of the chocolate cake. You can go back on the diet tomorrow."

If it isn't a spouse who sabotages you, it may be a "friend." I deliberately put that word in quotation marks because sometimes it is not until you try to reduce that you discover who your friends really are.

One woman I know lost nearly 80 pounds after being heavy most of her life. She was shocked by how many of her "friends" cautioned her against losing too much. They told her, "Now Sherry, don't get too thin."

I'm sure you've heard about those "friends" who tell you how bad or ill or haggard you look as you reduce.

Apparently, our associates are frequently more comfortable seeing us as we have always presented ourselves. That way we are not threatening them or their conception of us. They have compassion about their poor, fat friend who just can't help being that way.

As the saying goes, with friends like that, you don't need enemies!

I wish Jane's story had a happy ending but it doesn't. She died at the age of 32 from a ruptured cerebral aneurysm. Because she had been severely overweight most of her life and had suffered from high blood pressure, her entire body was under tremendous stress. Although physicians say aneurysms are congenital, you can't convince me that her obesity did not contribute to her death.

I wish I could brighten my story here, but I must make my point in order for you to understand what did and did not motivate me in my determination to stay thin for life.

To continue the family story—my father, as I mentioned earlier, was also very heavy. (By the way, when I say *very* heavy, I am not talking about ten or twenty, or even thirty pounds overweight. I mean much more than that. He was obese.) He, too, suffered from high blood pressure. At the age of fifty-one he, quite suddenly, suffered a fatal heart attack.

My mother, another victim of high blood pressure (don't forget she was barely five feet tall and averaged 185 pounds), suffered a number of strokes. At the age of sixty, she was more like eighty years old. She entered a nursing home, hardly able to walk and with severely impaired speech. Two years later she died of a ruptured abdominal aorta.

Wow!

I must admit, every time I think about it, the whole picture staggers me. It is quite obvious to me that because my family was chronically obese, they were prone to many illnesses. Experts keep reminding us. Dr. Theodore B. Van Itallie, director of the Obesity Research Center at St. Luke's Hospital Center in New York City, reports that "In countries where people tend to be fat, there is more endometrial and breast cancer—as well as more athero-sclerosis, blood lipid disorders, strokes, heart attacks, gout, and gall bladder disease."

The strongest connections are between obesity and hypertension and adult-onset diabetes. I don't know if my family was fortunate that it wasn't prone to diabetes; maybe they just didn't live long enough to get it! The con-clusion is obvious. Obesity can kill.

That fact scares me. And my family history scares me even more.

Whenever I have a headache—which is quite rare now that I'm thin (I used to suffer from them frequently when I was heavy) I immediately wonder if I'm next. If my blood pressure is slightly elevated, I become con-cerned.

I wish I could say that all this is why I decided to be thin, but that isn't the truth. The family story is an after-word to my own experience. And part of the reason I have described it is to illustrate a point: people do not reduce because of fear.

People don't get thin because they're afraid they're going to die.

Of course there are exceptions. People frequently do lose weight after they have had a heart attack and their doctor tells them if they don't get thinner, they will have another one. People go on diets when their blood pressure goes up, but most return to eating as usual once their pressure returns to normal.

You see, secretly we all believe we are immortal. We tell ourselves: "Everyone else may die, but death will somehow pass me by and I am going to live forever."

Absurd? Put down this book and think about it for a minute. Isn't it true that although rationally you know you are going to die, deep in your heart, you don't really believe it?

Sounds crazy, doesn't it? Well, psychiatrists tell us it's a universal craziness. Crazy or not, most people go through life believing "It won't happen to me." To other people, yes—but "Not to me."

Keep in mind that you are somebody else's "other people!"

Well, if fear was not the motivating factor for me, what was?

And, on this cliffhanger, let's pause for a moment.

Intermission

Two questions to ask yourself:

• **When was the last time you went on a crash diet so that you could fit into a special outfit, or because you were going on vacation and wanted to look good in a swimsuit?**

• **After the vacation was over, did you keep your weight down?**

3

Why and How I First Lost Weight— or, How to Stop Kidding Yourself

What is the strongest motivation for becoming thin? Obviously, this isn't a question that can be answered easily. And the answer will differ for each person. But you can find similarities among people and with that in mind, let's continue.

On a short-term basis, a strong motivating force can be a particular goal. In my case, the first time I lost weight was when I wanted to become a high school cheerleader. I went on a crash diet, lost about fifteen pounds and made the squad. I didn't stay thin for long. Once secure, I went back to the cupcakes and managed to stay on the cheering squad, too—a bit heavy in the thigh; but a cheerleader still.

My second short-term goal was getting in shape for my wedding. Actually, it was the need to fit into a borrowed wedding gown. The gown was quite beautiful, but the only way the endless row of buttons would close was if I got rid of about twelve pounds. I made it.

If I didn't have to return the wedding dress—or perhaps if I wore it daily—I might have kept the weight off. However, during the first year of my marriage, I discovered the joy of freshly baked apple pie and gourmet cooking and 11:00 P.M. coffee and cake.

I gained twenty pounds. Of course, my husband also gained twenty pounds, so who noticed? Moreover, it seemed to me that everyone around us was heavy.

At that time I never thought of myself or of my friends as heavy. Looking back, I can't believe the amount of food I consumed. Perhaps people were not as weight-conscious in the 1950's and '60's as they are now. At least my circle of friends was not.

If a woman wore a size twelve dress, she didn't consider herself stout. Today, fashion has accustomed us to dress sizes that top off at ten. On the down side, you can even find some women putting on size one. (Is anyone really a size one?)

Actually, a hairdresser at the salon I use is a size zero. Yes, "0." But she also has a tiny frame. Her two legs together look like one of mine.

And have you noticed how a new size is appearing in the shops marked "extra small"?

Frankly, I wonder if designers don't just label clothing with sizes smaller than they really are. They understand the psychology of female shoppers. Most women would be thrilled to fit into a smaller size than they thought they needed. I know that the first time I fit into a pair of pants marked six, I ran with my money to the cash register. I didn't care whether or not they looked good—they were a size six! And that meant I was skinny. I wouldn't be at all surprised if clothing was soon marked "small" "extra small" and "teeny-weenie."

Not everyone overweight admits to being uncomfortable about it.

There was a publication that claimed it was speaking for fat people. The magazine called *Big Beautiful Woman* resulted from its editor, Carol Shaw, being unable to find attractive clothing for her stout figure. She uses the term "fat" with no apologies. Though we may not all look like movie stars, Ms. Shaw stresses that "everyone— no matter what size she wears—is entitled to the most up-to-the-minute, fashionable clothes available."

Ms. Shaw started her magazine when she became

angry at the lack of appealing apparel for heavy people. While she does not promote fatness, she does advocate ending discrimination against fat people—especially women.

She—and others who followed—have had a great deal of impact. There are large models as beautiful as thin ones. There is more attractive clothing so you can dress well even if you aren't a small size. There are fashion shows featuring large women and I think that's swell.

On the other hand, clothing for the average size and thin people has gone to the other extreme. We have reached the point where our bones must be barely covered with flesh or much of the clothing we see for sale will not fit. Even the "roomy" things don't look good unless you are very thin. We are obviously manipulated by fashion towards slimmer and slimmer figures, no matter how we try to keep our weight goals realistic.

Let me illustrate—using women's fashion again, since it changes so drastically.

I don't know if you were around when skirts were tight and belts were tighter. I had a very wide leather belt that had a spiral closure. Once it was on, you needed to turn the spiral ever more tightly until you could barely breathe.

We used to push ourselves into skintight jeans, and then stand in the shower wearing them. After they dried they were even tighter. Pants were so slim that sometimes they had zippers at the ankle to allow you to get into them.

Time passed and fashion changed. Clothing got more comfortable and skirts weren't tight. Pants had nice wide legs—and even pleats at the waist—so that the size tens and twelves could occasionally fit into a smaller size.

More time passed and, as you can probably guess, we were back to tight jeans and skinny skirts. The pendulum continues to swing back and forth from tight to roomy to tight.

If you don't like what they are showing you don't have much of a choice because all of last year's fashions always manage to disappear each new season. And we model ourselves after the ultra-skinny mannequins who show off the new styles.

It's no surprise that we demand a thinner profile of ourselves than we did in years gone by. Now we want the clothing to look as good on us as it does on the models. I have concluded that I am now about as thin as I can get without fasting every other day. (This is quite different than the rationale I used to use when I was reducing. Then I used to believe I would faint if I didn't eat something every four hours. Or, I'd have headaches every time I started a diet.) Moreover, I am less interested in looking or being skinny than I am in having a well-toned, strong, body. Sometimes that means adding on a few pounds of muscle, but it doesn't have to change your dress size.

Happily, while being thin is definitely still "in," also growing in emphasis is the goal of being fit.

Years later, after I had reached my goal, I was sure that most of the symptoms people describe when they begin dieting were imagined. They were rationalizations, just like mine. All excuses to avoid dieting.

Imagine my surprise to learn that headaches are common at the beginning of a diet. That's right, you're not making it up after all, and neither was I.

A panel of physicians specializing in weight reduction was queried by the editors of Obesity/Bariatric Medicine magazine. The consensus agreed that many people do suffer headaches when they begin reducing. There are several causes, including emotional ones.

Emotionally-based headaches are the result of using food as a pacifier. There are also metabolic causes for headaches, such as low blood sugar (mild hypoglycemia) which is caused by the reduction in carbohydrates the body is taking in as compared to before the diet.

Sometimes, with the reduction of carbohydrates, the dieter experiences a sudden and severe diuretic effect. That's when the body loses a great deal of fluid. You know, that's when you're in the bathroom all the time. With the loss of fluids you can also lose sodium and potassium (one of the problems with the protein-sparing fast that was popular years ago). This is why it's important to drink a lot of fluids—preferably water—as you try to reduce.

I could describe clinically and graphically what happens to the blood vessels in your head, but it's sufficient to say you can end up with one whopping headache.

Whatever the cause, emotional or physical, it's a real headache you may be suffering. But hold up before you feel vindicated about abandoning your attempts at reducing because you can't bear the headaches. Please keep reading.

These same physicians agree that the headaches are only temporary. You might want to take an aspirin or Tylenol to relieve the symptoms. Or, if your headache is caused by low blood sugar, a teaspoonful of honey.

My book is concerned with taking weight off and keeping it off—in a healthy way. It's designed to teach yourself and your children good eating habits so that neither you nor they end up obese or anorexic.

I want you to lose all the weight you feel you should. You can learn to be sensible about food and not become undernourished. If you don't take precautions to eat foods that satisfy your hunger and keep your body in good health, you may find yourself thin, to be sure, but not feeling good.

Perhaps some of those people who provoke the comments about how bad they look thin may actually look bad, because besides limiting their calories, they may have also been short changing their bodies of vitamins, minerals, and the rest of the ingredients that keep human beings alive and healthy.

If your reducing program is sensible, you will look better as you reduce than when you were heavy. You can't cheat your body; the outside will reflect what's going on inside, for better or worse.

I make this point because there is a strong case to be made for the fact that although Americans may be eating less, they are ignoring nutrition. Moreover, as if things weren't bad enough, they are not necessarily losing weight.

We've become a nation of lazy people. On the one hand, we read about how many of us are exercising. On the other, Americans are more sedentary—and fatter than ever.

In spite of the popularity of fitness these days, putting on your running shoes once in a while isn't the answer. If you have a job where you find yourself sitting all the time, being a "weekend jock" simply cannot make up for the lack of overall exercise. The dieter's tendency is to decrease even further the number of calories to compensate. It doesn't work.

Keep in mind when you are being realistic about your weight goal, that when you reduce your caloric intake, you may also find you are not consuming the recommended minimum daily amount of nutrients. While your caloric needs decrease when you reduce, your nutritional needs do not.

I will show you how to discover when you've reached that realistic weight goal. Once you're there, I want you to be content with your weight, as I am.

I am happy with the way I look and feel. I don't want to go without eating—so this is it for me. But it wasn't always that way.

After my first year of marriage and the addition of those twenty pounds, I found myself lumbering along. I'm the type of person who gets heavy all over, so I convinced myself I wasn't heavy just because my employer teased me by saying he heard me clomping down the hall.

I found myself wearing a lot of basic black. Coco Chanel once sold fat people on the idea that the color black is slimming. Look around and you'll see a lot of large people dressed in black. Believe me, they are not all in mourning.

I also wore pleated skirts because some fashion authority once said that pleats hide fat. If anything, they emphasize it. You have to be very thin to wear a pleated skirt because the pleats are supposed to lie flat, not bulge the way they did on me.

Well, the high point for me (or low point, depending on your point of view) followed my first trip to Europe. In three whirlwind weeks, I gained fifteen pounds. I was eating constantly, and enjoying every mouthful. Each new city brought new taste delights. And I was determined not to miss anything. I don't think I did.

When I returned home, I was the fattest I had ever been! I could no longer ignore it. Nothing fit me. When I went shopping for new clothes, I couldn't believe the sizes sales people brought out. They couldn't be offering these to me? But they were.

I was *not* satisfied with my image. No matter how hard I held in my stomach, it still hung out. My thighs were chafed from rubbing against each other. My pants were worn out in the spots where my thighs rubbed together. My wedding ring was tight. *My shoes were tight!* (I went down an entire shoe size when I got thin!) Yecch! I hated myself.

I did the only reasonable thing under the circumstances. I went on an incredible eating binge. To soothe my hurt feelings about discovering the fat girl who stared at me every time I looked in the mirror, I ate more.

To add insult to injury, when I asked my husband if he thought I was too heavy, his response was not the one I looked for. (Naturally, I wanted him to be the mirror on the wall to my Snow White.) A bit reluctantly, but truthfully, he told me, "Well, to be perfectly honest, you *are* putting on weight."

That blunt answer supplied all the motivation I needed. My binge ended. Since my husband was also somewhat portly by then, we decided to diet together. This was very helpful because we gave each other moral support. If someone works with you, it can be an important factor for success.

We turned to Weight Watchers.

4

Weight Watchers—and Other Things to Watch

A t the Weight Watchers meetings I saw people who made me look like a toothpick, but I wasn't turned away for being underweight. We were all accepted.

We shared our stories and applauded each other's efforts. I heard more rationalizing about not being able to diet than I thought existed. Some pleaded that "the holidays are coming"—meaning they couldn't consider dieting for the period beginning with Thanksgiving through Christmas and New Year's. (With very little effort you could stretch this on to Arbor Day.)

Others said they couldn't possibly live without bread. Or pasta. Or mashed potatoes. All excuses. We found we could live without these foods, and we would live without them.

(By the way, today the Weight Watchers' menu has been expanded to include many of the foods which were excluded when I was on the program.)

I threw myself totally into the program, and went through Thanksgiving, Christmas, and New Year's successfully. As a matter of fact, I could have been up to my nose in cranberry sauce, but I wouldn't have eaten any of it to save my life.

I found the motivation of the group and the steady weight loss so reinforcing that I got more pleasure out of being able to say "no" when offered food not on my program than I would have had in eating it.

Although I was successful in reducing during the holiday season, this is an exception to the rule. I would advise you to be tolerant about your cravings during such times.

If your attitude is to maintain rather than lose weight during the holidays, you can face the New Year with renewed vigor towards your reducing program.

Eventually, I lost twenty pounds and reached "goal." I will forever be indebted to Weight Watchers for helping me.

I continued dieting long after leaving Weight Watchers, not because I was dissatisfied, but because their "goal" was just more weight than I wanted to carry.

I learned much about eating nutritiously from Weight Watchers. However, I also discovered a serious flaw in their program.

A Weight Watcher feels safety in the knowledge that there are some foods which can be eaten on an unlimited basis. These are the variety that don't add any weight, and may even be negative foods. (Radishes are an example. The red radish burns up more calories digesting it than it adds to your caloric intake.)

It's helpful to know that in an emergency—when you feel you must have food in your mouth—there are foods you can eat "legally." But if you follow the advice I offer, as you reach your weight goal, you will not only become a thinner person, you will also become a person who is in control of your food management.

You will discover that no matter how "legal" a food may be, there simply are times to eat and times not to eat. One of the keys to staying thin is managing this balance. By the time you finish this book you, and not your fork, will control when you eat.

The Carole Livingston Stuart approach will transform you from a person who thinks "fat" into one who thinks "thin".

INTERMISSION

•Think about one food that you have always considered forbidden—because you believe it makes you fat. Make sure it is something you really crave.
•The next time you want it, promise yourself to wait ten minutes (by the clock) before eating it.
•After ten minutes, ask yourself again if you really want to eat it. If the answer is yes, go ahead—and enjoy it.
•If the answer is no—you have just taken one giant step forward. Either way, you have made your own decision. The food has not decided for you.

Congratulations!

5

Thinking Thin

Thinking thin. Let me clarify this concept. When I was heavy—and even after I had lost those first twenty pounds—I felt secure knowing that if I got desperate I could eat some foods in quantities to pacify me. In those days I still believed I was a fat person lucky to be temporarily thin. I knew that eventually I would get fat again. I always did.

Most serious dieters are like this. As a matter of fact, like clockwork, every year (usually at the same time) they begin their diet. Then, they gradually put it all on again. And the following year, right on schedule, begins the diet.

At that point in my life I kept all my "fat" clothing because I knew I would need it sooner or later.

Later—much later—I learned that when I truly believed I was thin I didn't need the security blanket effect of keeping food ever present. I could do without food for a period of time. I wasn't going to faint if I skipped lunch. I learned self-control. (Remember that concept? when we are infants we have to learn self-control in toilet training, in not shouting out in class, etc.)

If we merely substitute "good" foods for "bad" ones we haven't yet learned that there are decisions to make about eating or not eating.

One of the reasons we stay fat is because we continue to cling to that infant-like belief that we just can't stop ourselves. That means you can eat and blame yourself, forgive, and go on eating because you have condemned yourself as weak-willed and a baby.

Overeaters also blame "outside influences" for eating foods in quantities they later regret. I used to do it all the time. For example, I traveled to work by subway. I took the same train to work in the morning and the same train home at night. Routine. But if anything disturbed that routine I would use it as an excuse to eat something I shouldn't. If the train was late, I "rewarded" myself for waiting. After all, it wasn't me who made the train late, so didn't I deserve some goody?

Sound familiar?

An important part of being thin is *accepting the responsibility* that you make yourself the way you are.

If you are fat, you made yourself that way. If you are thin, you made yourself that way, too. *Nobody else did it to you!*

Very simple—but a very difficult concept to truly understand and to make a part of yourself. I know this because it took me many years for me to fully comprehend it. After reading this, you'll be able to benefit from my experience and embrace this concept now.

When I accepted responsibility for eating or not eating, I no longer rewarded myself for late subway trains. On the contrary, I found myself passing up foods that I knew would make me fat. *My reward was in the knowledge that I could wait until I was able to eat to my satisfaction.*

I was proud of passing up these foods. I sympathized with those who made excuses, as I used to, about why they got fat again. "My mother insisted that I eat everything on the plate." "If it's there, I eat it." "If I don't eat it I'll hurt his/her feelings," etc., etc.

There's that infant attitude again. Getting fat is out of your control; it's something other people or outside forces do to you.

Stop kidding yourself. We do it to ourselves. Whenever someone tells me they can only diet if everyone around them helps out, I know that person is not accepting the responsibility for making his or her own decisions about food.

Taking this responsibility is not easy. (I never promised you it would be easy!) In fact, it's *very* difficult. But it is possible to accomplish. Only *you* put the food into your body and only *you* can prevent it from entering. You make all the decisions. Once you accept this, you have taken an important step forward.

Before telling you about what I did next, let me suggest five steps to prepare you for losing weight.

FIVE STEPS TO GET READY:

1. Get a notebook. This will become your food diary as described later in this book.

2. Mark the first page "Past" and describe your own history of being overweight. When did you begin to get fat? Why did you begin to get fat?

3. Mark the second page "Present" and record the ways in which you are keeping yourself fat. List all the foods that you can recall eating during the past twenty-four hours. List all the foods you eat today that are between-meal snacks.

4. Mark the third page "Future" and write down all the reasons why you want to become a thin person . (Not just "get thin" but *become* thin—and stay thin.)

5. Turn to page four. Record two numbers. One will be your accurate weight today. The second number will reflect the number of pounds you'd like to weigh one year from today.

Now put away the notebook and read on...

Liking Myself
(the Vanity Syndrome)

I t seems simple now, looking back, but it took a while
for the vanity syndrome to work for me. For quite
some time after I lost weight I did not give up my "fat"
wardrobe.

Holding on to "fat clothes" was the same as holding on
to the belief that inevitably I would get fat again.
However, the longer I remained thin—and got even thinner—the more I liked myself. It was also true that I felt
better, but it was the image in the mirror that really turned
me on.

My weight loss was achieved in stages. They weren't
planned stages. However, since they were gradual it gave
me a chance to become accustomed to the constantly
changing me. Whenever I reached a plateau and couldn't
get any thinner, *I concentrated instead on staying at that
weight.* As long as I didn't put on any weight, I was temporarily satisfied.

What I was not prepared to do at that time was to give
up a number of foods that kept unwanted pounds on me.
Compared to the "old" me, I was skinny. So I stayed
slightly overweight for a long time.

Speaking of plateaus, have you ever wondered why
two people who appear to be eating the same number of
calories don't always lose at the same rate? Generally the
heavier you are, the more weight you will lose. Some peo-

ple, however, do lose faster than others. And men lose weight with more ease than women.

This has nothing to do with liberation, ladies! It's biology. The Associated Press reported on research done at the Medical University of South Carolina where twenty-two men and eighteen women were studied for twelve weeks. On average, men lost fourteen pounds while women only took off seven. (The men started out averaging a weight of 230 against 176 for the women.)

Why? Well, the research team points out that "The body composition of males contains proportionally more muscle and less fat than that of females. Translated: men lose more rapidly.

If you keep that in mind, you'll never go on a weight loss bet with a man. And, you may have found at least one answer for an occasional plateau you reach, while the guy next door doesn't.

There were positive aspects of my plateaus. Although I wasn't as thin as I am now, I *was* learning to feel good about myself and my figure. And this helped build my self-esteem.

You can use a plateau positively to prepare yourself for the first time that you will again feel ready to reduce. Although part of this is rationalizing, part is being realistic. It's especially difficult to reduce if you are not positively motivated. As long as you promise to get back to the diet—maybe even by setting a date on your calendar— you will stay on a forward path.

My next dramatic weight drop was a positive side benefit of illness. Others have told me of similar situations. For instance, a good friend confided that although she had always been stout, during a brief illness she lost a great deal of weight. After that, a very unhappy personal crisis caused her literally to lose her appetite. Her depression was so severe that she simply couldn't eat.

I've heard people say, "When I'm depressed, all I can

do is eat." That's the case for many overweight people. But at moments of true despair, appetite often does disappear.

After her depression lifted, my friend decided to enjoy the ironic benefits of her misfortune. To this day she has kept her trim figure.

I do *not* recommend depression or deliberately getting ill as a realistic weight control device. I hope this is clear! If you find yourself thinner after being ill or glum, your body will need the nourishment it couldn't accept while you were sick in order to keep you healthy. Don't—I repeat, don't—go searching for a mild case of anything!

My illness happened to be a bad back. I found myself bedridden. For three weeks I was permitted to get out of bed only once a day.

I panicked. I was certain that having nothing to do all day but lie inactive in bed, I would again grow fat.

I was so upset by this possibility that I became compulsive about not eating any more than I normally would. As a matter of fact, I tried to eat less to compensate for lack of exercise. Unwittingly, I began using many excellent devices to stay thin and I've since learned these are often used by successful dieters.

Each morning, before my husband left the house, he brought to the bedroom, where I lay, all the food I would consume during the time he was away. I had a cozy little setup at my side, with a toaster oven, Thermos jug of coffee and so forth all within arm's reach.

Since I could not get out of bed, I ate only those foods that had been prepared ahead of time. I knew in advance what I was going to consume. I use this same principle successfully now.

Planning what you will eat before you eat it, helps to cut down on unconscious overeating.

At the end of my bedridden three weeks, I stepped on a scale and was astonished. I had lost five pounds! This proved to me that you don't have to gain weight when your daily routine is disrupted. Disruption is a great excuse—but only for those seeking an excuse to fatten up. (Remember I learned *not* to reward myself with food when the subway train came late.)

I learned that I really did have control over myself and I justifiably felt proud.

It would have been easy to say, "Well, I was in bed for three weeks and put on a little weight."

Who would blame me? Who would not sympathize with a bedridden person? But who is it you are trying to convince that you've done the right thing? Yourself, that's who. Instead of making excuses, I had turned my illness into a triumph.

By the way, before you get the idea that I have a will of iron, let me confess that along with self-control, I understood that I would be very depressed if I got fat while in bed. So I was protecting my emotional well-being as well as my figure.

As time passed, I began to replace my out-dated "fat" wardrobe with new clothing. I symbolically let go of my fat image by letting go of those clothes. With my new fig-ure, I wanted to reward myself —but this time it was with pretty things instead of with food.

As I shopped I was conscious of the considerable cost of buying new things. This pushed me into a syndrome that acted to motivate me further. If I was going to invest in a new wardrobe, I couldn't afford to replace it if I got fat again. Thus, more and more I found myself committed to my new figure.

The next stage in my weight loss occurred during and after pregnancy.

Once again, I was filled with anxiety about gaining extra pounds. I'd heard stories about women who had been skinny all their lives until they became pregnant—and then, the cravings were just too strong. One woman told me that during the last four weeks before giving birth, she did nothing all day but sit in front of her refrigerator and eat.

Was I going to go the same route? I remembered those three weeks when I'd been bedridden with that back injury. If I didn't use that experience as an excuse to get fat, I decided I couldn't use pregnancy either. Pregnancy, after all, is not a disease. Frankly, I never felt better in my life. I kept my weight gain within the limits suggested by my obstetrician and after Jennifer was born, I not only returned to my normal figure but dropped a few pounds to boot.

I reached the conclusion that just because some women get heavy during pregnancy, and stay that way later, doesn't mean that they all do. And I wasn't going to be one who did. By the way, you might look around and notice lots of women with children who are not fat. They obviously got through it successfully too. Others simply "use" pregnancy as the excuse to gain ("Hey, I'm going to be looking fat anyway, so what's the difference if I go crazy and eat more?").

The next period of my weight loss is most interesting and familiar to all of us. I wasn't ill, pregnant, or even very much overweight any longer. I was at that point many of you may recognize. I only wanted to lose another ten pounds.

After those ten pounds, I promised, I would be happy. then I would never have to go on another diet for the rest of my life.

Here, by the way, is a time during which dieting can become compulsive. Particularly if you're not very clear about your goals. the closer you get to your goal the more you may try to reduce just a little bit more, "for security." I found that when I lost even one "security" pound, I immediately considered this my new weight level. What had been intended as an extra pound under ideal weight, so that I might be able to overeat once in a while, quickly became absorbed in my thinking as my new ideal weight.

You will learn, as I did, to keep to you goal and not strive to reduce below it. Otherwise you are toying with compulsive dieting.

When I set about losing those last ten pounds, I was going through a divorce. (I guess you could say that when my husband and I parted I lost 185 pounds!)

There was no special drama connected to the dissolution of my marriage that sent me into the depths of depression. On the contrary, I found myself freed from schedules, especially those that meant I had to prepare breakfast, lunch, or dinner. Except for my toddler, I didn't have to cook meals if I didn't want them. And, I could eat what I wanted, when I wanted to. By this time I virtually had memorized calorie charts and knew what I should eat. I also had learned (thanks to Weight Watchers) a balanced approach to eating.

I decided to eat only if I was hungry and then, I would eat practically the same thing for every dinner. (I hadn't read about one-sided diets then. I had simply devised my own.)

Oh, there was a short period after the divorce when I ate on the run, or spooned tuna fish right out of the can in order to save washing dishes, However, after a while I found myself getting depressed. It didn't take long to realize the depression was because I had turned dinner from what should have been a pleasant experience into something mechanical and boring. For me this meant that eventually I would become careless about what I ate and that would mean trouble.

I deliberately changed my eating patterns. After all, wasn't I worth having dinner with? I liked myself and decided to treat myself that way. And so, every evening, at dinnertime (I use dinnertime as an example because I was away from home at work during the day), I would set the table for myself. I used a place mat and napkin—a real cloth napkin, not paper.

If I was having wine with my meal it wasn't in a grape jelly glass; it was in the best wine goblet I owned. Sometimes I ate by candlelight. And whether it was steak or hamburger, I sat down and enjoyed it. I ate my dinner at an hour when my daughter was happily occupied or, if that was not possible—and sometimes with children it certainly is not—I waited until she was asleep.

My attitude was totally pleasure-oriented. I made up my mind that if I was going to eat, I was going to enjoy it.

Before very long I had dropped those ten pounds. You may have noticed that throughout my story about losing weight, I haven't been very specific about what foods I ate or did not eat. I haven't told you what to eat or when. If I did that, this would be just another diet book. It isn't. Anyway, by this time in your dieting history you've undoubtedly read all about green leafy vegetables and the like. You know what you can and can't eat. And you also know that some things work for some people and some don't.

There is no diet, no form of weight reduction that will work for everybody, all of the time. That is why I could not successfully go back to Weight Watchers to lose more, even though it had worked for me once.

There is no magic, no pill you can swallow at night and wake up lighter the following morning (no matter how we wish otherwise, me included). And it's never easy. No matter what any book ever tells you, if they say it's easy, drop it like a hot 93-calorie potato.

Why do you think so many diet books are best sellers? They are bought by the same group of people—those perennial seekers of the magical weight-loss secret.

Save your money. This could be the last weight-reducing book you will ever need. Once you have made your decision to become thin—and stay thin—the next step is to realize that, simple though it sounds, it isn't going to be easy.

Yet, if you can channel the energy you once spent on buying pastry into feeling good about the change in yourself, you can be one of a very elite group. You may become one of the fewer than ten percent who reduce and continue to stay thin. Fewer than ten percent? A depressing statistic? Not if you are determined to be one of us!

Time to ask yourself once again: "Do I sincerely want to become thin and stay thin?"

If the answer is "YES!"—let's move along. Let's examine some positive and negative approaches to taking it off.

7

Getting Ready

The first step in losing weight isn't to read all the diet books you can find. It isn't going to the doctor. It isn't filling your house with low calorie beverages and throwing out all the pretzels.

The first step is admitting to yourself that you need to reduce.

I have met many people who look at me like they are in urgent need of cottage cheese and celery but you couldn't convince them. Somehow they ignore the expansion of their waistline and the need for extra holes in their belts. By the way, I'm not talking about a few pounds overweight, I mean h-e-a-v-y.

So, first of all, admit that the dry cleaner isn't shrinking all your clothes, which I once believed had happened to me. It was during a trip to Paris, after I'd spilled perfume on the trousers of one of my suits. Off it went to the dry cleaner. On getting the suit back, I was absolutely flabbergasted. Trying to get the pants on, I could not believe that the cleaner had not shrunk them. I pulled them off quicker than a wink and didn't dare to try them on for a long time.

A few months later (and a few pounds lighter) I casually pulled on the same pants. Not so magically, they fit. It is your body that is expanding—not your clothes that are shrinking.

The next step in getting ready to reduce is to decide not to indulge in self-pity about admitting to yourself that it is, indeed, necessary to reduce.

Self-pity is similar to hating yourself for being out of control. It only leads to food binges. Then you enter into a cycle that is difficult to break. Besides, self-pity is simply another method we all occasionally use to delay getting on with what we really want to do.

Okay—you've admitted you need to lose weight. And, you did manage to throw away part (if only a sliver) of that candy bar instead of devouring it entirely. Great! You're back on track. Now for the next step.

This step is an important one. It's when you must decide that today is really the day you are going to begin.

Really today.

Not a week from next Wednesday. Today!

Now. This minute!

I hear the voices already... "But I have to decide which diet to choose. "I have to shop for the 'right' food."

Sure, you will need to do all that. But you can do it even while you take your first step to the goal of a thinner you.

Impossible? Not at all. You aren't going to pass out if you miss a meal because you don't have the "proper" food in the house. (If you recall, I thought that would happen to me. I'm here to tell you it won't.) Honest. And among the foods already in the house, I'll bet you can find something "right" to eat even while you are making your plan.

When I visited the Pritikin Longevity Center in Santa Monica for the first time I experienced what I called "food panic." Part of my visit included cooking lessons and instructions on how to shop and how to "Pritikinize" my kitchen.

Many people don't even want to try the Pritikin diet because they think it's so difficult to stick to. Dean Ornish, using virtually the same principles that Nathan Pritikin originated took the concept even further. His program allows for no more than 10% fat consumption and is much harder to follow.

In truth, it does take a major reorganization of your approach towards food, but it's not all that hard. In the main, you stop eating as much fat as possible; cut down significantly on your consumption of cholesterol-building foods and increase the complex carbohydrates, veggies and fruits.

When you make the changeover you have to face throwing out a lot of things from your pantry and adding new ones. Thus, food panic. I felt frightened, truly frightened. What would happen to me between the time I arrived home after my two-week Pritikin stay and when I'd be able to hit the supermarket. After mulling this over, I realized that nothing would happen! Surely I could find something to eat. There must be some potatoes I could bake. And I had salad makings. And then I called upon my own philosophy: If I don't have the proper food, I can wait until I get it. And so can you.

When I first went on the Pritikin program it was not easy finding restaurants that would accommodate this style of eating. But today, even fast food chains are trying to offer lower fat foods. And I added three words to my restaurant vocabulary: "on the side." That means salad dressings, sauces, condiments, etc.

I have almost never been in the house of an overweight person where there wasn't a container of cottage cheese in the fridge. True, it frequently goes from purchase date to mold formation without being touched. But it's there. If it's still edible, eat it. If not, there's got to be something to eat—a can of tuna (drain the oil or better, keep water-packed instead); a slice of bread. You get the idea.

More important than what you are going to eat for your next meal—you have made a giant leap towards becoming thin!

INTERMISSION

Two Ways To Strengthen Your Resolve:

1. Say out loud, "Today is going to be the day I am going to change my eating habits forever." Do this before each meal.

2. The first time today that you're tempted to eat something you know you shouldn't eat, go into a different room and say out loud: "I don't need this food. I'm going to trade it off for my long term goal."

8

Planning

You've taken the step. Congratulations! What you have accomplished by deciding to get thin—for the last time—is to take your life in your own hands. You have made the decision to have control over food, and not the other way round.

The decision alone should make you feel exhilarated.

The fact is, at this point, you actually haven't physically done a thing. But do you notice that you feel a sense of accomplishment? That's because you are the boss now. There are few feelings that can beat this one.

I know this feeling so well that I want to pause here to assure you I understand intimately what you are going through. Whenever my weight begins to creep up I still have to go through the very exercise I've just described. I call it "collecting myself," just as a rider collects his horse before starting out.

Here's something you can try right this minute. Stretch up tall. When you walk, walk tall. You will feel better. Fat people slouch, thin ones don't. *Start thinking thin.*

I have taken a great deal of time describing "getting ready," because if you are not ready, nothing is going to work. If you are ready, just about anything will work.

It's that basic.

Okay, so you're ready. Now what do you do?

I would suggest that you make an appointment with a

physician for a thorough examination. This can never hurt. It also costs money, and for some people financial involvement is an important incentive toward weight reduction.

When you see your doctor, tell her that you plan to lose weight. After she stops applauding, she may make some helpful suggestions. She may even hand you one of those photocopied diet sheets we have all been given at one time or another. Remember, though, don't wait for your doctor appointment. That's just another delaying tactic. Today is the day, right? Right!

The fact is there really isn't any special preparation for dieting once you make a decision to do it. You can do it this minute. Recall my description of being a Weight Watcher during the Thanksgiving and Christmas holiday seasons? Remember, too, that I was so positively motivated that my exposure to many tempting foods didn't make me eat them.

The next suggestion is to read up on nutrition. The last time I had to learn about nutrition was in the Montauk Junior High School hygiene class.

There are any number of sources of information. Health-oriented magazines publish articles all the time with the latest findings. Your local public library also has a variety of books and magazines on the topic.

If you own a computer or have access to one and can go on-line, surf the Internet and find out what's the latest information. If you are going to lose weight effectively, you owe it to yourself to learn what proteins, vitamins, minerals, carbohydrates, etc. mean to your body.

There is an excellent magazine called *Nutrition Action* published in Washington, DC which gives a monthly update on what's "in" and what's "out." You can find it in your library and you might even want to subscribe.

You don't have the time? You're in a hurry to get on with it? If you've taken the time and money to invest in this book, don't stop at this point. Remember, your goal is to become aware of what it is that makes you fat. One step towards awareness is learning how the food you put into your body reacts once it's digested.

Planning helped me enormously. Whether you have a hundred pounds to lose or only a few, a plan is essential.

Remember those height and weight charts I mentioned earlier? Do you cheat, pretending you have a "large frame" so your ideal weight is higher than you know it should be?

If I could only have grown taller, all my problems would have been solved. After all, I was about the right weight for a woman of five feet, ten inches tall. Now that I'm slim I realize those charts can be a joke.

They merely act as a crutch to lean on.

The latest method of determining your weight to health risks is called Body Mass Index (BMI). Rather than simplifying things, it complicates them. You have to multiply your weight by one figure, your height by another and then square (I haven't heard that term since high school) the answer and divide. You end up with a number by which you can determine your risk.

Do you really need this? I don't think so.

When I got thin I never looked at a chart again. You know you're thin when you are. You can see it in the mirror. Charts are for people who want to convince themselves that they are not as fat as they know they are. Knowing you're thin is like knowing you've had an orgasm; if you only hope you've had one, you haven't. It's something you can't mistake. You can't make a mistake about being thin either.

Okay, so you have told your physician about your plan to reduce. You're going to become an expert on food values. Now tell your family and friends.

Tell your father, your mother, your mate, your co-workers, your dog. Tell everyone. Why? For one thing, you'll want to have them on your side. For another, the more people you tell, the more committed you will be. You don't want to humiliate yourself in front of everybody by failing, do you?

Through it all, you'll avoid being hurt by others' lack of interest if you recognize the fact that your dieting may be a compelling matter for you, but is not always of that much interest to the people around you.

Obviously, it's more important not to forget your promise to yourself. But let's be realistic. You want to have as much going for you as possible. Look at losing weight as a sort of war—and in war you use every weapon you can get your hands on.

Bear in mind that I'm the type of a person who benefits from sharing information. I guess that's why Weight Watchers succeeded for me. Organized groups of dieters such as Weight Watchers, Jenny Craig, Overeaters Anonymous, etc., are effective partly because their members share each other's dilemma.

They work because you admit that you need their help, and it makes the group feel good because you believe it can help. Also you can profit from learning by example. Everybody is working together.

You can even go on a cruise that is especially designed for slimming. This is quite a challenge because to many, a cruise translates as endless quantities and varieties of food and many pounds gained. It might be interesting to concentrate instead on the ports visited, lectures given and entertainment, instead of how many steaks you can put away at one meal.

Diet guru Richard Simmons runs such cruises all the time. Ask your travel agent if this interests you.

Now, if you are the type of person who does not benefit by sharing your weight reduction plans with others then just erase everything you have just read from your mind.

This book is about helping you to get thin. No single approach will work for everyone. I want you to get thin. I'm flexible, too. I am the first to admit I use many approaches to keep trim, sometimes changing from one day to the next.

Maybe you won't tell anyone (except possibly your doctor) that you are on a diet. This might sound like a contradiction but really it isn't.

I only advise sharing it with others if you believe it will help you get thin. For those who will not benefit from this, I will have lots of other ideas for you. For you sharers, stick with me as I continue a while longer in discussing the benefits of this approach.

Now that you are publicly committed to dieting and your family and friends are put on notice (reassured that you are serious about this) you can start to plan.

By the way, when you announce you're going to lose weight and you hear collective groans, knowing they are silently asking "again?," don't be discouraged. Admit to them that, "Yes" this is another—yet another—attempt to reduce. But this time you are going to do it until you get it right! If you can convince them that you need their help, they may stop groaning and start assisting. (As I suggested earlier, beware of diet saboteurs!)

Although I don't usually recommend negative reinforcement, this is war! Leaving yourself open to your friends' jibes and teasing when they catch you cheating can present quite a challenge. You are on the spot to prove to them (and to yourself) that you can stay on the straight and narrow. In any event, the winner will be you as the pounds come off.

Back to planning.

Now is a good time to decide how much weight you want to lose. What is your goal? Is it realistic? I mean, if you are a woman who is six feet tall, it's not very realistic to believe you can ever weigh 100 pounds—and stay alive. But then again, why would you want to?

If you are a male six-footer, don't shoot for 135 as a realistic goal. You can discuss goals with your physician. Or, if you must, go ahead and consult a height and weight chart. Get an image of what you want to look like. Then close your eyes and picture yourself thin.

The next step is to decide how long it will take.

Stop now and think about all the crash diets you have tried. Obviously, in the long pull they don't work, or you wouldn't be reading this.

Don't be in a hurry at this point. This planning step is a crucial part of your weight-reduction program. Being sensible about how much you want to lose, and how long you expect it to take is critical.

You must be realistic. Remember, you are now ready to give up the belief in magic pills and formulas. You didn't get fat overnight, so it's silly to believe you can take it off that way. (Read this paragraph a second time. Before you have finished reading this book, you will understand that it is a key to the ultimate secret of successful weight loss.)

There's another one of those deceptively simple sentences. You can read it and think you understand it. Take a moment now to digest the significance of what you've just read.

All right—you've decided that today is the day. You've told everybody about your decision (or you haven't, if you are the keep-it-to-yourself type). You've set a realistic goal and determined how long it's going to take. Now for the next step.

What Works and What Doesn't...Sometimes

What are you going to eat? What are you not going to eat? When, where, how are you going to eat? Don't panic. Let me tell you some of the things that helped me and some that helped other people. Let me also tell you some things that don't help. And let me repeat: nothing will work for everybody all of the time. And—IT'S NEVER EASY.

In the last chapter I devoted a lot of space to the "sharing" approach. I also allowed for those of you for whom that is the worst piece of advice. Perhaps you need to keep your diet to yourself. Maybe you couldn't bear to watch your friends anticipate another failure. (Or, perhaps you lack self esteem and enjoy the humiliation that fat and failure bring!)

What is most important is to understand your needs and to devise an approach that will work for you. It might be fun to surprise people with your weight loss. Obviously, those who see you frequently will notice after a while that you are reducing. They may ask if you are on a diet.

You can have some fun by pretending that you didn't even notice that your clothes are starting to hang on you. They'll think you have suddenly become a guru about losing weight, having quite unconsciously discovered the secret of true thin bliss.

If that turns you on, go with it. But be true to yourself and keep on the right path.

As we all know, some people will do anything to lose weight. Lots of people pay large sums of money to go places where they don't eat anything. Fast farms. They go into seclusion.

Although not as popular as they used to be, there are still many believers of fasting to reduce. You are fed juices, water, and virtually nothing else until the weight comes off. The people who run such places make most of their money on repeat business because nothing prepares you for going back to eating and having no such plan, the weight comes back—in a hurry and often extra pounds to boot.

Some people insist that they need an initial jolt to change their direction and an immediate loss to encourage them. In that case, fasting on a limited and carefully supervised basis can be helpful when you begin a new diet program. However, remember, eventually you are going to leave the fast farm and face the world of food again. Your scale may reflect an encouraging weight loss, but if you are not prepared to follow up with a practical approach to eating, you will be back in the same spot again before very long.

The same philosophy applies to any program that isolates you from the world.

Notorious publisher Al Goldstein once went to Structure House in North Carolina where they specialize in helping obese people reduce. After a stay of several months he reduced by more than 150 pounds! However, he didn't change the way he eats, which made him fat in the first place, and, you guessed it, he gained all the weight back.

More recently, he was taking Xenical, which is talked about as a breakthrough in medical treatment for the obese. You take this medication and lose weight. Sounds too good to be true? It is said to block one-third of the fat that is taken into the body. But it also cautions that it caused increased bowel movements, sometimes causing a lack of bowel control as well as other unpleasant possibilities. Al soon figured out the weight he was losing was largely due to the increased number of visits to the toilet. How much fat he lost along with the waste elimination is questionable.

Lyle Stuart, my husband and the publisher of this book, is a classic example of the "successful" faster who failed. Some years ago, he discovered the protein-sparing fast. He drove four hours for his first visit to the doctor who was administering it. Lyle wouldn't wait for the week necessary for the doctor to study the medical test results: he insisted on going on the protein-sparing fast that day. Immediately!

Lyle Stuart is a strong personality and the doctor couldn't resist his demand. The doctor put Lyle on the fast at once.

For 120 days Lyle didn't swallow anything but water, a pink protein liquid, and some vitamin tablets. During this time, he took groups of people to the finest restaurants in Paris and New York. He hosted banquets at his fabulous home in Port Maria, Jamaica. And while his guests feasted, he fasted, showing off by sipping his pink liquid.

Some people marveled at his determination. Others cautioned him with "If you don't eat, you'll die!" or tried to discourage him with "you look terrible."

Actually, he looked different—but he looked marvelous. As a result of his personal experience, he persuaded the doctor to produce a book called *The Last Chance Diet*. It was an immediate best seller. It became the diet book of the year, in time selling more than two million copies in all American editions. It was published in Germany. It was published in Holland.

And Stuart himself? After 120 days, he lost 83 pounds. Eighty-three pounds in 120 days! incredible. He flew to Rome and had his tailor, Angelo, make a complete new wardrobe for him. He stood at his company's exhibit booth at the American Booksellers Convention in Chicago, displaying himself in front of a poster of the old, fat Lyle Stuart.

He had gone from 240 to 157 pounds.

There was only one thing wrong. True, the compulsive eater had become a compulsive non-eater. But now the fast was over. He'd reached goal.

Lyle Stuart broke his fast at that Bookseller's Convention party where they served Guacamole and chili and enchiladas.

He loved 'em. He always loved 'em.

So he ate. And ate. And the next afternoon he returned to the same hotel suite, where they were again offering Mexican food, and he ate and ate and ate.

You see, nothing had changed. His eating habits were no different than they had been before the fast. They'd merely been frozen. And now when they defrosted, he did what he'd always done.

He ate.

Today? Well, I can tell you that he has a closet full of never-worn elegantly tailored custom-made suits by Angelo of Rome.

Crash diets don't work except temporarily. Drastic weight loss will be followed by drastic weight gain.

The unhappy fact is that most people find they not only gain back all the weight they have lost, but many add a few pounds as topping.

Even more discouraging for the crash dieter is the phenomenon that occurs with subsequent attempts using the same crash method. The fact is, your body doesn't know how much of its fat is "good" and how much is "bad." And being a pretty intricate unit, it does its best to

try to hold on to all of itself. It becomes thrifty. It mani-
fests that thriftiness by developing a resistance to the same
crash methods. Each time you try the same crash diet it
will work less and less effectively.

One woman, who had crashed dieted away eleven
pounds in one week, found that, a few months later, using
the same diet, she could take off only five. Her body had
become thrifty. That doesn't happen when you reduce
slowly and sensibly.

You don't really want to establish crash dieting as a
way of life, do you? Be realistic this time.

Many people who can afford it go to lavish spas where
they can be massaged and pampered while taking off
unwanted pounds. Many celebrities seek sanctuary at
such places as the Golden door, La Costa (another spa,
also in southern California), Canyon Ranch (either in
Tucson or Massachusetts. There are many and they can be
located in a guide called "The Spa Finder."

The total environment of a spa is quite appealing, and
the food in very low calorie and low fat portions is beautifully served.

Such spas do indeed sound attractive. You might look
upon visits to spas as luxurious vacations, for that is the
category in which they deserve to be placed. Even if you
could afford La Costa or the Golden Door or other spas,
the time comes when you must leave. Then you have to
face reality and make food decisions on you own. So
enjoy the spas, but don't think of them as a solution to
staying thin.

Ask yourself: "Am I willing to accept the reality that
losing weight is not easy?"

Are you finally willing to accept the fact that there are
no miracles that will make you thin?"

Take an honest inventory of all the dreams, wishes
and desires related to the idea of miraculous weight loss.

Reveal to yourself these self-defeating illusions, and

then move past them into the reality of a daily weight loss and maintenance program.

Intermission

As part of your reducing program, read at least one item about nutrition. Whether it's a chapter in a book an article in a magazine or on the Internet, promise yourself to learn something that you didn't know before about food and how it is used by your body.

10
Diets, Diets, Diets

The protein-sparing fast Lyle Stuart tried was developed some years ago in research directed by Dr. George Blackburn, associate professor of surgery at the Harvard Medical School. It was very popular although not many people use it today. However, it's worth mentioning because many "new" weight loss programs are merely polished up, recycled versions of earlier ones, so this may resurface in some form or other.

Lyle Stuart's experience doesn't mean that the protein-sparing fast isn't effective. It can be, under controlled circumstances. Dr. Blackburn, together with Dr. Peter G. Lindner of South Gate, California, ran a program that involved 167 grossly obese patients. When it ended, Blackburn reported that eighty percent of his patients had been successful in reducing their weight; the average loss was 40 pounds, and those who followed the basic rules of the program stayed trim for the year or more the were monitored by watchful physicians.

The important ingredient that accounts for the success of these patients, and that was lacking for Lyle Stuart, was behavior modification. Without it, almost all of the people would regain the weight. With it, they were able to learn how to stay thin. Again, they had to change their eating habits on a long-term basis, not a temporary one.

Unless you decide to work closely with your physician. or nutrition counselor, don't consider this program. A further caution is that the protein-sparing fast is not a diet for people who have less than twenty pounds to lose.

I add that last comment because you may be thinking the same thing that I thought on hearing of the diet. At the time I had five pounds to lose and thought I'd go on the modified fast and drop them quickly. I wouldn't have to be concerned about planning my foods, etc. Did it work? Not for me. I simply didn't have enough weight to lose.

Which brings me back to my often-repeated point: not every diet will work for everyone.

In describing the protein-sparing fast I emphasize the inclusion of behavior modification, if the weight is to stay off.

Behavior modification is one of the most important concepts in weight reduction success. As most of us know (because we've done it lots of times), it may not be easy to lose weight; but it's even more difficult to keep it off. Actually, behavior modification is merely a new name for what people have done for years; Whether you call it relearning, re-education, changing your habits—it all adds up to altering the eating habits that made you fat.

First, of course, you do have to get the weight off.

Since we know by now that each person will respond differently to each approach, it's important that you find the way of reducing that you can live with. There's no point in eating grapefruit and peanuts for three months (sure, you can reduce that way, if you don't eat anything else) if you are not prepared to eat that way for the rest of your life. You must examine your current eating habits to discover how to design an approach to weight control that will be effective and realistic.

Boredom is the major ingredient in most of the one-sided diets. Whether it's protein-sparing, any single food diets such as eating hard-boiled eggs, or rice, or bananas, or grapefruit, you frequently lose weight because you quickly become accustomed to the regimen and aren't particularly interested in overeating when you are limited to the few foods the diet allows.

A big problem of one-sided diets is poor nutrition. Though you may be losing weight, you may not be eating well enough to provide your body with the day-to-day vitamins and minerals it requires to keep you in good health.

The most impractical feature of one-sided diets is that they are aberrations. You aren't going to eat in that way for the rest of your life. So once the diet is over, you go back to old eating patterns and get fat again.

One-sided diets are all too often crash diets, and we know now that these not only don't work, but work less and less each time you try!

Some eating approaches aim at both reducing and good health. Certainly with the introduction of so-called natural and unrefined foods, more people are genuinely interested in combining weight loss with a healthy outlook.

Suddenly we started to hear about fiber. If you didn't include fiber in your diet, you were on the wrong track. Bran as a fiber source started selling like crazy.

What is fiber?

Well, the definition of fiber may depend on who is doing the defining. Traditionally, fiber is the leftover part of a food after it has been treated with chemicals that are similar to those which are involved in digestion. Or, to put it more simply, fiber (or dietary fiber, which is the term used these days by nutritionists) is the portion of the food we eat that is not digested.

With people now worried about dying of colon cancer and heart disease, there's a strong appeal to a food, whose increased quantity in our diet could aid to prevent such illnesses as well as diseases involving the lower intestinal tract. Fiber may be linked to the advice our grandmothers gave to eat an apple a day to keep the doctor away. Lately, however, the cancer-fighting benefits of fiber are in question.

Fiber is a bit more complicated than the above abbreviated description, but essentially it entails adding bulk to the diet. Since so much food we buy is refined practically to the state of mush, bulk, if you want it, has to be added back.

Fiber does two things—first, it absorbs water in the intestinal tract and causes you to have a bulky soft bowel movement; second, because the contents of your digestive tract are now bulkier, your excretions are speeded up. That's why fiber (such as bran) has a laxative effect.

If you believe the theory that the longer food stays in the bowel, the greater your chances for getting diseases like cancer, you'll think fiber is great. Get all that stuff out quickly. If the new theory is correct, we can all forget about fiber. At least for its anti-cancer focus.

What is the appeal of fiber for us dieters? Those who praise its use feel it encourages weight loss. Some of the over-the-counter diet aids produce a full feeling in the stomach, with the promise that this will discourage eating. It would appear that using fiber to give a bloaty feeling is not a new idea.

Scientists are naturally skeptical. Some caution against too much fiber in the diet, especially if you have colitis or diverticulitis. Surely fiber would aggravate these conditions on the other hand, since we eat so many processed foods and refined grains, maybe we could add a little fiber to our diets.

Those who are in favor say it's difficult to eat too much fiber. Because you do feel fuller when you add bulk to your meals, you'll just stop eating when you have that bloated feeling. Obviously, this ignores the fact that most overweight people eat well past the point where they feel full. That's why they are fat!

When the positive effects of bran in the diet first became widely acknowledged there was concern about their being a shortage of bran on the market. Imagine! A shortage of bran. Why you probably couldn't give it away during the years before we started to hear about its "miracle" qualities. And that's what every fat person is looking for—a miracle. Something that will replace his own effort in reducing, something else that will cause you to drop weight without having to go hungry or feel deprived.

I don't really want to burst your balloons, but I do want to help you become an aware human being who won't always be sucker for the next "cure" to come along.

By all means, add fiber to your diet. Keep your colon clean. Can't hurt. But don't expect to get suddenly thin because you are adding it to you diet. Add it but stick to whatever method you use to reduce.

The important point to keep in mind is, once you are thin, you must learn how to stay thin. And be assured that this book will help you, if you want to be helped.

Getting thin is only Act One.

My first success came through Weight Watchers. This works for lots of people and may work for you. It undoubtably accounts for the longevity of the program. A similar group approach is used by Overeaters Anonymous which I mentioned briefly earlier. There is a sharing of experiences and information and an intensive support system for people who admit they have a compulsive eating problem.

Overeaters Anonymous (or O.A.) does not prescribe specific foods to eat. Rather, they try to help members discover what drives them to eat compulsively. Like Alcoholics Anonymous, they employ a sponsor relationship in which members can call upon one another for support when they feel they are about to go out of control.

Many members feel that they have found people who

understand their eating problems at O.A. meetings. Some
have said that even their families, who try to understand
their overeating, can't compare to fellow members who
truly know what it means to go wild with food. Who have
experience anxiety so unbearable that all they can do is
think about eating.

If you think Overeaters Anonymous might be right for
you, check your local telephone directory to see where
there is a branch. The organization is nonprofit and has
been very effective for those who pledge themselves.

After completing the Weight Watchers program, I
found it difficult to return to that method later on in life
when I wanted to lose weight. I had to keep finding new
ways. I no longer got as turned on by the group approach
as I had earlier. By the way, this is not the case for everyone so I don't mean to discourage you if you are a veteran Weight Watcher and want to return. Their program has
changed a lot since I was a member and it is still one of
the most effective methods of weight control.

I consider myself a successful Weight Watcher because
I will always carry with me many concepts I learned
under that program.

I also tried fasting and for a while this worked. I ate
moderately all week long and then let loose over the
weekend. Desserts are my passion, so, from Friday night
until Sunday night I allowed myself anything I wanted.

I must admit that this program was fun. At least for a
while. I'd indulge all my sweet-tooth desires: cookies,
cakes, muffins, I had it all. But on Sunday night it all had
to go. Ironically, it all went-right into me. It never
occurred to me that I could have thrown the uneaten
goodies away! Of course more often than not, there
weren't any leftovers.

On Monday morning, all the cakes and munchies
were gone and I would fast all day. I later named this
approach to maintaining my weight the "feast or fast"

method. By the way, pay attention to the word "maintain" because that's what you do: you manage to keep to one weight. This doesn't get you thin.

Fasting wasn't difficult after eating a large quantity of sweet foods. I was so bloated on Monday mornings I had little appetite. Moreover, I usually had a rotten taste in my mouth and felt physically under par too. That discouraged eating. Years later I recognized that I was reacting negatively to all those sugar-laden foods.

What I was experiencing, without realizing it, were food hangovers triggered largely by the abundance of sweets I had eaten.

If you want to learn more about the effects of sugar on the body, read the classic book, *Sugar Blues* written by William Dufty. Dufty, who was really obese, met actress Gloria Swanson. She converted him to a healthful diet. She was way ahead of the times in her thinking about food. He became thin and the contrast was so great that old friends literally didn't recognize him on meeting him! He married Gloria Swanson.

If you find yourself reacting oddly when you eat sweets, it may be that sugar and you are not meant for each other.

Today we are starting to understand that sugar can not only make you fat, it can make you ill. We observe the behavioral changes in children after they have consumed large amounts of empty-calorie foods loaded with sugar. But in the past, if ignorance was not exactly bliss, it kept me sweets-satisfied.

I managed to keep my weight pretty much at the level I wanted it. For a while. Before long, though, I found it becoming more and more difficult to discipline myself and Mondays would occasionally slip by without fasting. The dial on the scale started to move up. I had to change my behavior pattern unless I was prepared to get fat again.

I changed.

11

Uppers and Downers

Maybe you have thought about taking diet pills. There is a man I know who had been heavy most of his life. He went to a doctor who prescribed diet pills. The pills we are talking about are all variations of amphetamines—sometimes called "speed" or "uppers."

Amphetamines must be very carefully administered by a physician to avoid addiction. Not only is a tolerance built up by the body, meaning that larger and larger doses are required to do the job of curbing appetite, but it's also very difficult to stop using them as they're physically and mentally addictive.

Doctors who casually prescribe amphetamines have been dubbed "Dr. Feelgoods." The reason is obvious— amphetamines give you a feeling of euphoria. It's not easy to stop taking a pill that makes you feel good.

Before finishing this story I must go on record and say *this is a very dangerous way to lose weight.* In fact, the government has taken steps to ban the use of amphetamines in weight reduction programs altogether. However, for the man I mentioned above, diet pills were effective. He used them as a crutch for about six months and lost a lot of weight. That was quite a few years ago and he is still thin.

This fellow is the exception—not the rule. People usually deceive themselves while taking the pills into believing they are on their way to becoming thin. In reality, the pills can work against you because they don't require you to use any will power in resisting food. Your hunger symptoms are artificially masked. Once the effect wears off you often find yourself hungrier than ever and eat twice as much as you might have under ordinary circumstances.

I admit to having taken diet pills on occasion many years ago. And I'll tell you the truth: they don't work. Not only did I find myself eating uncontrollably once the pill wore off, but when I considered my weight over a period of several months, I had accomplished absolutely zero. I was exactly the same weight as I had been, before the pills.

More importantly, I found my heart racing, my memory disappearing and my mood increasingly irritable. Equally upsetting was my tendency to hoard my diet pills. I held onto them, just in case I would not be able to get a new supply. What I didn't realize then was that this behavior similar to an alcoholic hiding a bottle of booze—"just in case." This was very self-destructive behavior.

No pills for me.

If you think there is a way around the prescription drug route by taking products sold over-the-counter, don't kid yourself. Although non-prescription diet aids are not as potent as those needing a doctor's prescription, they can be strong enough to have ingredients that require caution.

If you read the ingredients on the labels, you'll see that caffeine is frequently mentioned. If you believe caffeine acts as a temporary appetite depressant, you can save your money and simply brew a pot of coffee.

For those still not convinced that amphetamines are a "no-no," let me continue. Most of us are not on the mailing lists to receive the magazines our doctors read. In those targeting the bariatric (diet) physician you find pages of advertisements for various substances that promise to help patients suppress their appetites.

One such ad was a beaut. I won't name the pharmaceutical company or the product. But it was for an amphetamine.

Nearly the entire ad is devoted to warnings, precautions, adverse reactions, and overdose information. If you read that tolerance to the drug usually develops within a few weeks, you might still decide to use it for a short period. But if you knew that it is ill-advised to drive a car while taking it, or that you ought to be cautious even if you had only mild hypertension—or you might get palpitations, insomnia, even psychotic episodes (though a rare reaction) or diarrhea, etc., etc.—you might (I hope) decide against it. Although this information is included with the product, doctors often remove it from their prescription packages.

If we had a chance to read all the facts we'd probably swallow a lot less medication. Today's ads for medication are required to include such information. If you see products advertised in magazines whether for diet aids, heartburn relief or anything else, the following page is filled with highly technical data which most of us don't read, but should.

When I read that amphetamine ad I became frightened. But forget fear. We all know that fear isn't a strong motivating factor in weight reduction. The fact is, as I said, these pills just don't work in the long run. I discovered that. I hope I've saved you the trouble of finding this out for yourself.

One of the recent diet drugs was "fen-phen," a combination of two drugs: fenfluramine and phentermine. People went nuts over this drug because it seemed to be the answer to every fat person's dream. No serious side effects and the weight came off with very little effort. At least that's what was believed.

About 6 million people took this drug between the 1970s when it first appeared and 1997 when the FDA pushed for its withdrawal. The FDA cited the fenflu-ramine in connection with potentially fatal heart valve damage although the drug company that manufactures it denies the link.

Whether there is a link or not, the company recently lost a $23 million verdict to a woman who claimed her heart was weakened after taking the drugs for more than three months. She developed a rare and usually fatal lung disorder called primary pulmonary hypertension.

Please note that this drug had been around since the 1970s! As of this writing, however, it has been taken off the market. If it were still available, I'm sure many people would take the risk of serious illness and even death, hoping it would be the answer to their weight loss prayers.

But it's far better to accept reality that the only real weight loss will be controlled by you. And you'll have the thrill of knowing that the your achievement is through your own effort rather than from medication.

We must learn to recognize the signals our bodies send us telling us we are hungry. Once we do, we'll be better able to learn how to control ourselves. Eventually, we must develop improved eating habits. Hunger pangs are a phenomenon some fat people never experience. People eat largely out of habit, in response to appetite, because they are bored, because they are upset or anxious or depressed or angry, etc. But rarely do heavy people eat because they are really hungry.

After I had lost a lot of weight, coincidentally, my work changed and I found myself traveling a great deal on business trips. Danger! I was on a speaking tour and often did not have a chance to eat regular meals. Moreover, I was unfamiliar with some of the cities I visited and I was not carrying any "emergency" food with me. (You know what that is, right? It could be non-spoiling nutritious snack foods such as raisins, pretzels, fruit, etc.—even a box of dried low-fat cereal.)

For me, carrying emergency food began when I still believed I would starve to death if I didn't know when my next meal was coming. Later it became a realistic tool. If I have good snack foods handy when I'm traveling they will often help me overcome moments of hunger when I might otherwise lapse into uncontrolled eating.

Another habit I developed when I travel is to use a two-pronged approach for traveling by air. I always call ahead and ask what special meals the airline offers. You'll be impressed by the variety some carriers have. You can sometimes have a long list of alternative meals ranging from kosher to Hindu to lacto-vegetarian.

I ask if they carry Pritikin Program food. Usually, they don't, but I hope that if enough requests are received, one day they will. Failing that, I describe my food needs: low-fat, low-sodium, low-cholesterol. If they can't accommodate me, I can always opt for a fruit plate. Or, I sometimes order a seafood plate. Shellfish (the usual offering) is high in cholesterol but low in fat, so I treat myself.

If you've ever offered a special meal on a plane you'll notice that the food you get is usually more appealing than the stuff coming from the regular menu. Other passengers look at you with envy, wondering why they didn't think of it themselves. Actually, more people *are* doing it and "special meals" are more and more common on flights.

Better choices are also getting more common too— usually there is a vegetarian choice along with the usual fare. But paradoxically, while food choices are improving, getting served any food at all is getting scarcer. Airlines are cutting back on serving anything on short flights, and hotels sometimes offer boxed lunches for their clients to carry onto the flight with them.

Of course, there are frequent screwups and the food you order often doesn't make it to the plane. Or you may order a vegetarian meal and find it swimming in fat.

(Vegetarian does not mean low fat or low cholesterol.) Or, instead of a lovely fruit plate, the flight attendant puts an apple, a bunch of grapes, and a banana in front of you. Not bad, but no meal.

At that point, my second front appears. Out comes my shopping bag full of goodies. These can be fat-free muffins, salt-free pretzels, a bag of carrot sticks, fruit, a sandwich of my own ingredients, a salad - you get the idea. Occasionally I'll have a combination of airline food and my own.

You can always skip the food and just ask for the setup. That's the tray and silverware, cup and napkin so you can eat your own food without being a total slob.

My husband used to make fun of my food-carrying habits, but now I think he secretly appreciates the fact that "Carole the squirrel" will always have something stowed away—just in case.

◆◆◆◆◆

One evening I was on a book tour in a strange city. As I waited to be interviewed I began to feel grouchy and tired. My host hadn't eaten dinner and invited me to join him for a quick meal. The quick meal was a sandwich, the first one I'd eaten in years with two entire pieces of bread. Within a few minutes I felt revived. Afterwards I reflected that this may have been the first time in my adult life that I had experienced true hunger. This was a valuable lesson; the opportunity to experience the effect of food as an energy source. Food can be so pleasurable we forget the satisfaction it provides as fuel.

I'm not suggesting that you wait as long as possible before eating. On the contrary, don't starve yourself. When you are extremely hungry it's difficult, if not impossible, to be selective about the food you eat. However, you might spend a few moments thinking about the last time you really allowed yourself to get hungry.

I have discovered that my energy level is especially

high just before I find myself so hungry I cannot think of anything except food. My body operates most efficiently when the food is just about all absorbed. Ivana Trump is supposed to have said that she feels powerful when she's hungry. From the lean look of her, I'd say she's hungry often.

This malaise is the opposite of the natural energy you'll be tapping into. If lunch time is at noon, and you've had breakfast at 7:30 or 8:00 A.M., observe how you feel about 11:30 A.M. (provided you haven't eaten anything since your morning meal). It's an interesting exercise. Try it.

I'll illustrate this by giving you a reverse example. After a big lunch, it's hard to go back to work. It would be more natural to curl up into a little bundle and sleep. Countries where the siesta is practiced are those where the midday meal has traditionally been the largest. And, quite intelligently, in those countries, people rest afterwards.

◆◆◆◆◆

Now is a good time to discuss portions of food.

One of my favorite pastimes is reading restaurant reviews. Years ago, a widely-known food critic described the portion size in one restaurant as "gross." Too much to eat! At that point in my life I couldn't imagine how anyone could give me too much to eat. On the contrary, if I read about such a restaurant I would immediately plan a visit. Then too, my favorite eating places were those that served buffet-style meals and encouraged you to go back as often as you liked. When they saw me coming they knew profits would be down that week.

Well, time has passed and now I understand about "gross" portions. The first moment I found myself saying "There's too much food here" I understood that food critic. As you read this you may not believe that there will be a time in your life when you have the same reaction.

Believe me, it's true. I never thought it would happen but it did. And it can happen to you too. I'm reminded of the Woody Allen line when he complained that he was at a resort hotel where the food was lousy and the portions too small.

I enjoy food more now than I ever did when it was quantity rather than quality that interested me. I also have discovered that recipes indicating that four pork chops serve four people aren't really crazy.

Americans eat too much. That's how we got fat in the first place. Ironically, the harder we try to lose weight the fatter our nation has become. Our bodies need very little fuel (food) to keep running efficiently. I find that the less I eat (within reason, of course) the better I feel. I'm not suggesting that you starve yourself. But you should begin to think about how much food you are putting into your body.

I didn't get thin because I wanted to eat less and feel better. Not at all. But I did discover that I function well on small amounts of food; amounts so small that in the old days I would have doubted that they'd keep me alive.

When your next meal is in front of you, think about what you've just read. Look at your plate. Is all that food really for you? Or, should it be feeding your entire family? Be honest now. If you decide it's a proper portion for one, eat and enjoy it. But if you've begun to absorb some of what I've been saying, maybe, just maybe, you will push a teeny bit away. If you do, I know you are going to feel good about it later.

That leads me to a helpful reducing "trick." An acquaintance whom I hadn't seen for several months had lost a lot of weight. When I asked how he did it, he said he simply ate exactly half of whatever was put in front of him. Simple enough.

I tried this but I confess it was and still is very difficult for me to leave food on my plate. Therefore, even as I give you this trick, I remind you that it may not be helpful for you. (One more time—not everything works for everybody.)

If you think you can handle this approach, try it. Results can be terrific and preparation is non-existent. Just eat half of everything on your plate. However, if you find yourself eating the icing half of a chocolate cake, you've missed the point.

If you don't want to divide by two, just try eating less. A good friend who has successfully kept her figure told me, "I eat less of everything. I don't want to give up mashed potatoes, so instead of a cupful, I have a teaspoonful. It's enough to satisfy me."

Someone else I met invented his own way to control what he eats. He designed a dinner plate with lots of small round spots on it. He doesn't take the first bite until all the food has been fitted onto those small areas. By this time, he has lost much of his appetite. And he has insured that he will be eating small portions, since the food must fit onto those spots.

It works for him.

Well, my trick was sweet-tooth connected. I would eat a piece of candy just before mealtimes. (I ignored my mother's voice, which nagged at my conscience about ruining my appetite. My goal was exactly that—to try to ruin my appetite.)

I found that for a while at least, the candy was very helpful. I had to exercise a measure of control in order to limit myself to just one piece of candy, not the whole bagful. For insurance I carried precisely the amount of candy with me that would get me through the day. I guess that's why eating only half of what is on my plate doesn't work for me. I'd have to cut the portions in half before putting them on my plate for it to work for me!

The candy worked because I examined both my needs and my limitations. And that's what I'd like you to do. I'm not suggesting that you run out and fill your pockets with candy. Rather, think not only about what I did but *how* I did it.

As I said, eating half my food doesn't work for me. I guess as a child I was taught too well to clean my plate. Thus, if I carried a pound of candy in my pocket I wouldn't be able to use this trick effectively either. So, I disciplined myself by carrying only the amount of candy I need. That way I also removed myself from the temptation of eating more.

Being on a diet is tough enough. You don't have to walk through fire to prove you can do it. Keep tempting foods away. I knew myself well enough to know that once I got hungry I would eat everything.

Candy may not be a good thing for you. Maybe it would trigger you to eat out of control. Maybe carrot sticks in a plastic bag will work. Or two pretzels before lunch time. It's more important to pay attention to how I used the snack. Then you can apply that principle to some other food. Above all, you must learn to be completely honest with yourself about whether that item is going to help you, or whether you are merely looking for an excuse to eat.

You may believe you are honest with yourself. But remember when we discussed being honest about admitting you needed to lose weight? We all deceive ourselves from time to time. I delayed admitting I needed a diet until my husband told me that I was bursting at the seams.

Honesty with yourself is one of the most important ingredients for success in losing weight, and I will refer to it often. You must be able to look at yourself, and understand and accept your strengths and your weaknesses. I'm not talking about how strong you should be; I'm talking about how strong you are. We are all subject to temptation. Whoever denies this is not being honest.

Who ever said we have to be perfect? If you believe any human being is perfect, you must still believe in the tooth fairy.

Successful weight reduction does not come from being perfect. It is a result of understanding why you eat, and being realistic most of the time about how you are going to manage to keep yourself from eating things that make you fat.

I have been telling you how I got thin and stayed thin. And if you have been reading carefully, you have noticed that I never told you it's because I control my food desires all the time. Rather, I am leveling with you about my stumbles as well as my successes.

Being honest with yourself is more important than broadcasting your weight to your friends, spouse, or doctor. Sure, they can help, but in the final analysis they aren't lugging around the excess pounds. You are. And they aren't the ones pushing excess food into your mouth. You are. So, if you're serious about wanting to take off weight, and keeping it off, this is one of the most important concepts for you to digest.

Re-read the above paragraph and then put the book down for a few minutes and think about it.

Okay—now ask yourself this. Are you ready at this point in your life not only to take off weight, but to plan realistically how you are will eat in the future? Are you fed up with diets that don't seem to understand that you get hungry at 10:00 p.m. and not at 9:00 a.m.?

Are you ready to understand that it's going to take lots of effort but that the rewards will be worth it? And do you really accept full responsibility for all the food you put into your body? Because no matter what the outside pressures or temptations are, the truth is that you respond to those pressures and temptations by eating. You shovel food into your mouth. There are other ways to respond.

As soon as you accept total responsibility for your own

actions, you can make conscious decisions about altering them.

Remember, this is the turning point—the time of your life when you are about to change forever from a fat person into a thin one. I don't do it for you. Your doctor can't do it for you. Nobody but you can do it for you. And you can do it!

I did!

Now put this book down and review this chapter in your mind.

INTERMISSION
Nine Commandments for Weight Control:
1. Think of yourself as a thin person.
2. Plan your meals and snacks: know ahead of time exactly what and how much you will eat.
3. For the first week avoid all restaurants.
4. Do not read or watch television while you eat: concentrate only on your food.
5. Never eat anything while you're standing up.
6. Set your fork or spoon down after each mouthful. Don't refill it until you've swallowed.
7. Chew slowly. Taste what you eat.
8. Fill your plate only with the amount of food you want. Do not eat from platters on the table. No seconds.
9. Always leave at least a little food on your plate.

12

More Help

You and I are doing magic together.

Are some of the tricks I've shared with you tricks you already knew? Was there at least one that is new to you? Good. Then I'm helping. I don't expect you to come to this book a "virgin". But do come to it with an open mind.

I repeat: one approach will seem tailored for one individual's success, while another person might find the same technique utterly frustrating and self-defeating.

Let's look at an example. Some years ago a reducing food called Metrecal was put on the market. For those of you with short memories, Metrecal was a concoction of vitamins, minerals and a measured quantity of calories. In the beginning it came as a powder and you had to add water and mix your own liquid nourishment.

Metrecal had the advantage of being a complete meal in a glass for those who didn't want to bother putting together their own menu of nutritious and weight watching foods. It came in a variety of delicious-sounding flavors like strawberry, Dutch chocolate, and coffee. Metrecal was followed by many imitative controlled-calorie preparations. It was the prototype for similar calorie-controlled products like Slim-Fast, Optifast, and other meal-in-a-can diets where all you have to do is add water to the powdered potion.

A woman I knew really got into Metrecal. She learned to love its flavors. She used it faithfully. The only problem was she wasn't losing weight. When queried as to how she used Metrecal (which, after all, contained a controlled number of calories) she insisted that in the morning, every morning, all she did was drink Metrecal. When pressed, she reluctantly added one additional item of information. With the Metrecal, she ate a large piece of Danish pastry.

Examine the "diet" foods that you are eating if they don't seem to be helping. Could it be that you are supplementing too?

My friend the late Bill Gaines, publisher of *Mad* magazine, also used Metrecal. But he did it a bit more creatively. By the time he became interested in Metrecal it was available in premixed, measured portions in cans.

He, too, loved the flavors. His trick was to put the cans into the freezer. When he was ready to have his Metrecal he opened the top of the can and spooned it out, pretending it was ice cream. You can be sure it took a lot of time and effort to dig out the contents. Thus, the Metrecal portion went quite a distance, and satisfied his need for "dessert."

Since Slim-Fast was the most popular meal-in-a-can available when I had a few pounds to lose, I decided to try it. After all, I saw their television commercials with personalities like Tommy Lasorda and Ed Koch. Even Kathy Lee Gifford and her husband Frank told me how they "took it off" the Slim-Fast way.

It was a tough choice to make: Ultra or Regular? No matter. I mixed the powder with skim milk and drank it down. But it went down so fast I had no sensation of having eaten. So then I mixed it in my food processor with ice cubes, the end result being a huge amount of puffed up Slim-Fast that sort of resembled a malted.

The problem with this concoction and me was that it

filled me up with so much air that I burped from one Slim-Fast meal to the next. Also, I was obsessed with the idea of food. And I was still hungry. Slim-Fast was not for me. I missed food too much.

Speaking of foods that are labeled "diet—are they really worth it? I used to buy diet cookies and diet candies. The amusing thing I discovered is that they often aren't much lower in calories than non diet items. Read the caloric content of some of these so-called diet items and you too may be surprised to learn that a plain cookie has fewer calories than the one you have purchased as a substitute. And be assured, you'll pay a lot more for the diet cookie.

Even the Weight Watchers prepared frozen dinners sometimes contain more calories than a meal you can put together yourself. For far less money, too.

Lean Cuisine frozen dinners are another of the many prepared "diet" foods marketed to tempt us. It was revealed that the reason Lean Cuisine dinners qualify as "diet" food is not because they are especially low in calories, but because the portions are small and therefore manage to keep the calorie count down. If you read the labels carefully, you'll also find them relatively high in fat and sodium.

I reached a point when I decided that if I felt eating cookies was putting pounds on, I shouldn't be looking for a low-calorie substitute. I should be looking for a way to live without them. At least until I felt I had learned how to introduce cookies into my life without consuming more than I planned to eat. Then I would eat cookies and enjoy them. And everyone knows that non diet cookies beat the taste of sugarless any day of the week.

As for Bill Gaines, who liked to think of his Metrecal as ice cream—he readily admitted Metrecal didn't compare to the real thing.

One more suggestion if desserts are your passion: eat

yours as your first course. That way you'll really enjoy it and probably not eat more than your portion. You might even save a taste for last, and so start and end your meal with dessert!

◆◆◆◆◆

Exercise is an excellent way to help you reduce. If you already play tennis three times a week, chances are you are already fairly trim. But if you are more than just a few pounds overweight, and your idea of exercise is getting up to get another beer from the fridge, you may believe you don't have the energy to exercise. Or, you may feel defeated even before you begin. Don't be. No matter how modestly you begin an exercise program, get started. If you sit all day; stand up more. If you almost never walk; walk a little. Just start doing something.

My husband is considerably overweight. Okay—to be completely honest, he's obese. He accepts the importance of exercise in a reducing program, so he bought himself a treadmill. The best one he could find. Most of the time it's covered with his clothing or newspapers. But when he does get on it he admits he has more energy and feels much better about himself than when he doesn't. And that good feeling starts his day off on the right food foot too.

When I first lost weight I had no regular exercise program. I concentrated exclusively on food. Then I visited the Pritikin Longevity Center. There I learned that exercise is as important to food control and good health as eating properly. I found that if I exercised daily—or at least five days a week—and stuck to the Pritikin diet, my body was like an efficient machine. Exercising had become that secret ingredient that made the difference. It does increase your body's ability to burn calories. And ironically, you can eat more and lose weight. And once you've reached your goal, you can still eat more than you thought was possible and keep your weight under control.

At first, I confess, I took my exercise program like a prescription. I'd do it dutifully and was grateful when it ended. Gradually, however, I realized how good I felt afterwards. (I suppose it's the endorphin high that athletes describe.)

Now it's a rare day that I don't either speedwalk, get on the Stairmaster, exercise bike, treadmill or take an aerobic dance class. It has given me an additional benefit (as if slimness and cardio-vascular fitness aren't enough!): I have more energy than most people I know who are sedentary. And I often outlast my daughter, Jenni, when we take an aerobic class together.

I also have learned the benefit of weight training and try to work out with a trainer or on my own twice a week. As we get older it's important to keep ourselves strong, and our bones from becoming brittle. Moreover, as you build up muscle you will find that your body gets leaner, even if the scale doesn't show a weight loss. That's because muscle weighs more than fat. But best of all, working out with weights increases your metabolism and you can enjoy your food and not worry so much about gaining weight.

Many people worry that exercise will increase their appetite. I find (and many others with whom I've spoken agree) the opposite is true.

If you think lifting weights is only for young people, you are wrong. It is important at any age, and maybe even more important the older we get. For the elderly, having strong muscles and bones can be the difference between being wheelchair-bound or being able to lift yourself to a standing position and being able to get yourself to the bathroom. As you approach your seventies, eighties and nineties, see if this is a small consideration.

Recently I have being taking Tango lessons. At first it was just for the fun of dancing. But I quickly discovered how physically challenging dancing is—and it doesn't get boring. I am so exhilarated at the end of a lesson that I literally have no appetite. It's as if the challenge and excitement have filled me up. Frequently, I use that feeling after the lesson to skip a meal.

After analyzing this reaction I came to the conclusion that part of the fulfillment is from being totally involved. Ironically, there just are too few times when we food-oriented people find ourselves feeling that way.

So much in daily life revolves around food. We meet for dinner, we discuss business at lunch, socialize over cocktails. It's downright antisocial to suggest to friends that we simply want to meet and share their company, without involving food or drink.

Try to change the focus in your life away from food. It would be easier to resist eating unnecessary calories if they weren't there in the first place.

As for becoming totally involved, if you think about the way you spend your time, you'll find too few moments when you are so immersed in doing something that you aren't planning your next snack break.

Wouldn't it be interesting to consider those moments when you are so occupied? Then you can start planning to increase the time you spend productively in nonfood pursuits so you can increase their frequency.

When my husband was on his protein-sparing fast he was amazed by how much free time he had since he wasn't spending any time eating. I'm not suggesting you give up eating, but think of the things you enjoy, and do more of them.

If exercise is something you enjoy, get more involved in it. But, go easy. If you ordinarily do little more than lift yourself from your chair to change the station on the television tube (and alas, most new sets don't even require that: you lie there like a lump and just push buttons) get a medical checkup before you begin jogging several miles a day.

Studies show that "fidgiters" tend to lose weight more

effectively than those who barely ever move. So, if you are at the bottom of the exercise ladder, merely moving around, even a little bit, will make a difference.

Before you begin any strenuous exercise program you must make sure your body can handle it. Certainly, if you are carrying around a great deal of excess weight you especially want to make certain any change in your physical activity won't overtax your body.

If you want to exercise but believe you can't find the time or place, try jogging in place in front of your television set. Or, do ten jumping jacks while you're waiting for the elevator to reach your floor. (Make sure you're alone!) How about dancing around the house? All of these activities not only get your body moving, but acts as antidepressants. They are great methods of letting out emotions that are bottled up within us.

Barricade Books publishes *The Lazy Person's Guide to Fitness,* a book that will guide you gently into exercise if you are an absolute beginner. Remember, any movement is better than none.

There is one form of exercise anyone can do. And before belittling the benefits, remember, it is better than nothing at all, and requires little or no preparation. And best of all, it's time spent away from food!

The exercise I refer to is walking.

You'd be surprised at how few people there are who walk. Or maybe you wouldn't be surprised. Begin by walking a few minutes each day—perhaps instead of driving to one destination. A side benefit of walking is that you will find yourself examining your surroundings more carefully than you probably have in years.

If you really get into it, you might find yourself working up to walking an energetic mile daily. (That's only four times around a quarter-mile high school track.) Even if you don't change your food consumption, this alone should cause you to lose 10 pounds in a year.

"Roving" (actually brisk walking) was recommended by Nathan Pritikin, widely-known for his best-selling book, *The Pritikin Program*, co-authored with Patrick M. McGrady, Jr.

One of Pritikin's outstanding successes was Eula Weaver, a woman over eighty who entered the program with a history of incapacitating heart problems. After a year of diet and exercise she discontinued the eight medicines she'd been taking. After two years on the program she was jogging and riding a stationary bicycle. She eventually won gold medals in mile and half-mile events in the Senior Olympics held in Irvine, California.

Are you about to tell me that the above description has exhausted you to the extent that you will hang up your jogging shoes forever? Or worse, never buy that first pair? Do you completely reject the idea of regular exercise? Don't! Anything is better than nothing.

One important point: you must employ an aid in order for it to help, because just thinking about it is not the same as doing it!

You might try cooking. Cooking? Wouldn't that put you in the very path of temptation? Odd as it seems, some people find that they can spend hours preparing elaborate meals for their family and never eat a bite. I, too, have discovered that occasionally the preparation of food "fills" me up. Whether it's the aroma of food cooking or, again, the involvement in the activity as an art, by the time the food is on the table I often feel like I've already eaten.

You might observe too that many professional cooks, cookbook writers, and food critics are quite thin. They have learned how to live with food as their life's work and not get fat.

On the other hand, there is the woman who was so much of an unconscious nibbler that she found it necessary to wear a surgical mask in the kitchen so she would not feed herself. Even so, from time to time she would find herself trying to pass bits of food through the gauze!

So before you embrace this as a good idea, consider whether you are unconsciously seeking another excuse to get close to food.

If cooking turns on your appetite, obviously it isn't for you. In which case, remove yourself completely from food preparation. True, if you are responsible for preparing the meals for your family this isn't always easy to accomplish.

If you have youngsters who are old enough to help out in the kitchen, this might be the perfect time for them to learn how to cook. You can turn their lessons into benefits for you. All the mistakes they make while learning may bring food to the table that is easy to resist. And that means less food going into your body.

For those of you who live alone, here's another suggestion. Train yourself to shop only for the exact amounts and kinds of food you are going to consume. Take a list with you. Buy nothing that isn't on your list. This will cut down on impulse shopping. Forget about bargains for a while. Many such bargains are on large or economy-sized items. You may be saving some pennies, but you will be spending them on unwanted calories.

Learning how to shop while trying to reduce is important. If you keep in mind that supermarkets are designed to lure you into impulsive food acquisitions that you hadn't planned to make, you'll find it easier to resist.

It's probably not news to you that when you go shopping you usually end up with much more than the one or two items you planned to buy. Notice, when you are in the store, how most candy is placed at a five-year-old child's eye level. This is not pure accident. See how easily they can reach and grab a candy bar and then beg you to buy it!

When you're at the checkout counter you frequently find yourself waiting on long lines facing a tempting candy bar display. This goes for health food stores too.

The fact that a candy bar is made with honey or brown sugar doesn't help the dieter.

Okay, so how can you fight it? I've already told you to prepare a shopping list before entering the store. You've got to be able to develop a plan equal to the von Clausewitz strategy of war. It's you against them. The supermarket is enemy territory.

Why let yourself be tempted by seductive packages? If you must have snack foods, limit yourself to those you can eat without going crazy. If you can't resist eating an entire bag of peanuts, don't buy the bag.

Of course, there is another point of view about snacking. If you decide that you would rather forgo tickets to the next Super Bowl than give up your between-meal snacks, you could find things at the supermarket that are nutritious and not total calorie wasters. This will take a little effort.

Not all dieters will have the patience to prepare snacks from elaborate recipes. All too often we find ourselves wanting a snack "right now," and few will head to the kitchen to start cooking.

Whether you are cooking your snack foods or shopping for them, be sure you make conscious decisions.

One other suggestion about going to the market. Never shop for food when you've been shopping for other items. And never go shopping when you're hungry. You will be tired and tempted to "reward" yourself with food because you have been on your feet all day.

Don't keep food around "just in case" someone drops in. If your friends visit you only for the cake and cookies you serve, let them adjust to your new lifestyle. Genuine friends will support your efforts. And it will give you a chance to begin changing the focus of your socializing from food to people.

Tell your friends they can count on you only for coffee, tea or low calorie beverages. If they need to nibble, let them bring along the things they want to eat. Or, ask them what they like; have them on hand for the visit, and then make sure they take the leftovers home when they leave.

Another word about goodies. (Or should we refer to them as "baddies"?) People who have young children often use the kids as an excuse to stock supplies of Oreo cookies, chocolate bars, caramel popcorn and such junk foods in the pantry. As I discovered from doing this myself, my daughter Jenni not only didn't need the Lorna Doones and Hershey Kisses, she actually preferred fresh fruit. I was the one gulping down most of the empty calories, not Jenni and her friends.

Jenni grew up without a house filled with empty calories. She didn't miss them because most of the time they weren't there. Further, her school requested that parents not send the kids to school with lunch boxes filled with such items.

Most school food programs have gotten smarter about providing children better lunches than were served in past years. Many communities are making strides towards dumping the empty calorie foods from school cafeterias and bringing in nutritious items.

Food attitudes have evolved, even if eating habits haven't quite kept up with information. Schools, airlines, restaurants, are all offering healthier, lighter choices. But it's still your choice to make. To borrow Nike's motto, "Just do it!"

13

Dieting is Hard Work

You and I know that dieting is hard work. The very idea of beginning a new reducing program is enough to depress some people and set them off on an eating spree. But this isn't the start of a new diet; it's the beginning of your new life.

Taking responsibility for your life can be quite a turn-on. Getting thin will give you a rich sense of accomplishment.

This time you can win the war against fat—and not just the battle to take it off. I told you before: This is war. Think of your diet aids and controls as weapons in the struggle. Change your weapons from time to time if it will keep you from becoming bored. Boredom is a danger signal for dieters. It ranks with anxiety as one of the two most dangerous anti-food-control bombs.

Just as not every reducing idea will appeal to everyone, varying those which do help is also a good idea. I change my "weapons" often. Something that might have been a terrific idea last month may not help me to battle the temptation of those potato chips tonight.

The deep satisfaction that success brings can carry you through stressful periods of your life, and no longer will you misuse those moments to succumb to self-destructive food gorging.

Most of us know all too well how anxiety leads to overeating. It probably accounts for hundreds of added pounds. Perhaps you'll be inspired by the story of a woman I know who handled stress and weight control in a special, productive way.

This woman had gone through a year of constant changes in her life. These were both emotional and physical. In fact, in the period of one year she became deeply involved with a man and moved across the country to Oregon to be with him. By the end of the year the relationship had ended and she moved back to New York. During this time her career underwent several changes, and as her income level changed, she moved from one apartment to another.

I did not mention at the beginning of this story that the woman was overweight. Of course, you knew that. However, during this period she had been losing weight—more weight than she had ever been able to lose in her life.

When people are under the kind of stress I've just described and they are also trying to reduce, few have the determination to keep going. Ironically, when I asked the woman how she had handled her weight during this time, she told me that she had not only managed to keep from gaining, she had reduced even further.

She explained: "Since I had very little control over much of what was going on in my life, I realized that the one thing I could control was what was going into my body."

Dieting gave her a sense of control and success.

This story can be an inspiration if you're a person who grasps for every excuse to get off your diet.

Lots of us like to look to famous people for inspiration. From time to time we read how a movie star keeps his or her figure. I'm fascinated by these articles. It's always interesting to learn new methods. But there's also a certain satisfaction in discovering that even the rich and famous have weight problems.

Actress Angie Dickinson makes a strong impression. She says that one trick she uses to curb her appetite is to brush her teeth frequently. Now maybe it's only a publicity story, but I do it and it helps. You might try it too. Naturally, we don't want to whip out our brushes at the dinner table or in a fancy restaurant. But this might be the secret you've been waiting for all your life.

I have a firm rule: in the evening, after I've flossed and brushed my teeth, no food will pass through my lips. Since it takes about ten minutes to attend to my oral hygiene routine, I'm not going to eat something and then have to do it all over again. (Okay, so I'm compulsive about my teeth, but if it helps keep a rein on my food intake, is this bad?)

Let's keep our methods somewhat sensible, not like that of the woman who once confided that her secret was never to swallow anything. She carried a Styrofoam cup with her and after chewing her food thoroughly, she spit it into the cup. I suspect she "ate" most of her meals alone.

There are enough ways to cut down on eating without resorting to antisocial behavior. Your goal is to learn to live with food and be in control of what you eat, not to entirely eliminate food from your life.

Another widespread unconscious habit among dieters is to "forget" some of what we have eaten.

Early in our marriage, my first husband tried to reduce. I occasionally asked him what he had eaten that day. He dutifully recited it all. But it wasn't all. Too often he conveniently "forgot" the apple pie and coffee he had around mid-afternoon.

Here's one way to make yourself more acutely aware of what you put into your mouth.

Write down what you eat and when you eat it. At first, don't try to change your eating patterns. What you want to accomplish initially is becoming conscious of them.

Carry a notebook with you and each time you put anything in your mouth, write it down. Record it, even if it's only a stick of sugarless gum or a peanut.

Don't skip anything!

Be sure to note the time you eat. I'm aware that this exercise, if carried on too long, could become a pain, so let's limit the time span. But do it for at least three days.

Then study your records. If you have kept them faithfully you should see a pattern emerge. As an example, here is the record of a friend who took my suggestion and did exactly this:

DAY ONE:

8:00 A.M.	•1/2 cup of orange juice
NOON	•chicken thigh and leg in a tomato and eggplant sauce (approx. 1/2-3/4 cup of sauce)
3:00 P.M.	•1 cup frozen vanilla yogurt (maybe more)
6:30 P.M.	•2 vodka gimlets undetermined amount of Fritos
7:30 P.M.	•Chinese/wok style chicken with zucchini in a hoison sauce •1 1/2-2 1/2 cups salad: Boston lettuce, 1/2 tomato, cucumber, scallion, bottled dressing, •1/2 bottle white wine.
9:15 P.M.	•1/4 sliced cantaloupe
10:00 P.M.	•2/3 pint vanilla ice cream

DAY TWO:

8:15 A.M.	•1 cup orange juice, 1 cup coffee
4:00 P.M.	•undetermined amount(but not that much since I polished off most of the bag the day before) of Fritos •2 cans of beer
8:00 P.M.	•three pieces of cheese mushroom and pepperoni pizza, •club soda

DAY THREE:
(a terrible food hangover)

7:45 A.M. •1 cup coffee, black, no sugar

12:30 P.M. •small salad—iceberg lettuce, 1/2 tomato, 1 tbs. Bermuda onion, bottled dressing

5:30 P.M. •1 scotch sour (made with lo-cal sour mix and a spritz of lemon juice to make it palatable)
•a few nibbles of Fritos

9:15 P.M. •approx. two cups of wok-style shrimp dish—tomato paste, scallions, ginger, some brown sugar, soy sauce
•1/2 bottle dry white wine

DAY FOUR:

8:30 A.M. •1 soft-boiled egg,
•1/4 cup of orange juice
•1 cup coffee black

NOON   1 small slice of ham
•1 cup coffee

5:30 P.M. •1 bourbon sour (not made with lo-cal sour mix)

7:00 P.M. •salad—iceberg lettuce, 1 large mushroom, some tomatoes, oil and vinegar dressing chicken in white sauce with artichoke hearts, 1 stalk broccoli
•3 glasses dry white wine

8:00 P.M. •Several more cups of coffee

Keeping in mind that the purpose of reproducing a real food record is to make you aware of food, let's analyze my friend's record and see what we learn.

First, this is a person who enjoys food. Enjoys it enough to cook and vary the menu a great deal. It is also the record of someone who enjoys wine and cocktails, but not especially desserts. My friend eats balanced meals but occasionally nibbles more than desired.

There's a lot that can be modified. Don't forget this list does not reflect weight-conscious eating. It's simply a record of everything eaten, without dieting.

Now the time comes to ask yourself, if this was *your* food chart what would you suggest if you wanted to design a reducing plan, keeping in mind your food desires and your weight goal?

My recommendations? For one thing, I would simplify the recipes. The more ingredients added to a dish, the more difficult to keep track of the calories. At restaurants I tend to avoid foods when I don't know what goes into their preparation. (At home you can keep track, but nevertheless, elaborate combinations can easily add up to more calories and fat than you want to eat.)

Cutting down on added fat, will certainly result in a weight loss. As we've learned, foods high in fat will keep us fat.

In a comprehensive study conducted in China by Cornell University of the relationship between diet and the risk of developing disease, it was observed that in China, obesity is more related to what people eat than how much. In fact, the Chinese consume 20 percent more calories than Americans, but we are 25 percent fatter. When Jane E. Brody reported this in *The New York Times*, she pointed out the Chinese were observed to eat one-third less fat than Americans do. In contrast, they eat twice the amount of starch. So carbs are not the culprit, fat is.

There is a problem, however, if you plan to increase your intake of Chinese food trying to eat a diet similar to that of Chinese people. In this country, much Chinese food is fried and contains a lot of salt. The food here has been altered to cater to the American taste—and thus is much less healthy.

Although medical authorities urge Americans to consume no more than 30 percent fat, this may not be low

enough to lessen the risk of heart disease and cancer. As I
mentioned earlier, the Pritikin and Dean Ornish programs
reduce fat even further—to around 10 percent.

◆◆◆◆◆

Back to my friend's food report.

Next, I would suggest that my friend cut down on
alcohol. Not only does alcohol add huge numbers of calories, but it can stimulate the appetite so that you can lose
control over eating. (That could be the reason the Fritos
were eaten.)

Note that I didn't suggest cutting out the booze altogether. Chances are that would produce a feeling of
deprivation which might drive one further into eating.
Just cut down.

Incidentally, there is strong evidence that moderate
intake of alcohol may protect against heart disease.

It's inconclusive whether red wine is preferable to
white or if the alcohol in beer or spirits is as effective.
However, most important is the word "moderate."

And moderate means one to two glasses of wine a day,
at most. Six ounce glasses. Spirits would be less; perhaps
a one two ounce drink. Or one twelve ounce bottle of
beer. For more specifics, discuss the details with your
physician or nutrition counselor.

Becoming aware of what you eat is a giant step in
changing your eating behavior. Only when you are aware,
can you modify. If you never become aware, you'll continue the same patterns that caused the problem.

14

Conscious and Unconscious Eating

SEVEN STEPS TO GAIN CONTROL OF WHAT YOU EAT

1. For three consecutive days, write down everything you put into your mouth. Estimate the quantities. Record the time.
2. At the end of the three days, put a check mark next to those foods which were high in fat, in sugar, in sodium.
3. Circle cakes, candy, ice cream and other desserts.
4. Ask yourself if you truly enjoyed eating every one of the checked and/or circled foods.
5. Rewrite the list, cutting out at least two things on your list.
6. Ask yourself if your new list won't give you as much satisfaction as the list of foods you actually consumed.
7. Prepare a menu for the next twenty-four hours and stick to it.

I can't overemphasize the importance of becoming aware of the food you eat. Let me tell you about a friend who thought he knew what he ate, but really didn't.

During the day and throughout dinner Dan Gardner ate moderately. He couldn't understand why he had a large paunch where there previously had been a flat stomach. He thought about the foods he ate each day and his eating was certainly reasonable.

Dan was truly perplexed.

He discussed the problem with his wife, Joan, and she agreed to try to help him by observing his habits.

It didn't take long for Dan's wife to solve the mystery. Each morning, a lot of food was missing from the refrigerator. She noticed this before, but since Dan and his wife had two teen-agers, she assumed that it was their "growing children" who were snacking after dinner.

Dan's wife questioned the children. They assured her they weren't raiding the fridge. And so she confronted Dan with the obvious solution: he had eaten the food himself.

Dan thought about it. He was a modest eater at meals. But late at night, usually after Joan had fallen asleep, he would get out of bed and wander into the kitchen for a "light bite."

The fact is that somehow, in Dan's perception, the food he ate at night "didn't really count."

Dan worked with the book advertising department of *The New York Times*. He dealt with complaints, crises, deadlines and a bucketful of anxieties all day long. And he handled them well. But somehow they ganged up on him at night when he was lying in bed.

Joan decided to investigate. One night she pretended to be sleeping. A half hour later, Dan arose. He seemed to be sleepwalking.

Joan followed Dan down the stairs. She waited until the refrigerator door opened and closed. Again and again. Then she burst in, to a very startled husband. He was into a huge sandwich—a hero roll piled high with a little bit of everything!

Dan expressed such innocent surprise that Joan knew she had a real problem. Like a stubborn alcoholic, Dan couldn't relate his growing paunch to "his little occasional late night snacks."

It took weeks of soul-searching for Joan and the children to come up with a possible solution to keep Dan from becoming a baby elephant.

They decided to secure the refrigerator.

They hired a locksmith who gave them a chain and a hefty lock. Each night after dinner, Joan would chain the refrigerator door and lock the lock.

It worked!

Very quickly Dan shed weight. The paunch became smaller. It seemed as though a happy ending was in view.

And then, without reason, Dan began to balloon up again. And in the mornings, when Joan undid the lock and chain, there was food missing from the refrigerator shelves.

The family was faced with a new mystery.

This one was solved with logic.

Dan was no Houdini. He obviously had discovered where the key was hidden.

Again Joan did the "make-believe-you're-sleeping" number. Sure enough, twenty minutes later Dan was on his way.

The key had been hidden under a can of Comet scouring powder in a closet.

What to do? Joan confided the problem to a friend. The friend made a suggestion.

The next night when Dan reached under the Bon Ami can, instead of a key, he found a note. It read: "Not tonight, Danny Boy! The Phantom strikes again!"

It was signed by the friend who'd made the suggestion. Dan was so frustrated, upset and angry that he confessed that he was tempted to make a 2 a.m. telephone call to the friend to tell him off!

It's an amusing story, but I must point out that what Joan did in locking the food away was a short-term, not a long-term solution. Nobody can do it for you. *You have to want to do it for yourself.*

Are people often unconscious of their eating? More

often than you might imagine. I recall the story of John MacArthur, who was one of America's first authentic billionaires.

MacArthur could have bought almost anything he saw. His vast holdings exceeded those possessed by kings of old. And yet, deep down, he was still the insecure little boy who had run away from home.

One symptom emerged when he attended a party. Before he departed, MacArthur would literally stuff his pockets with the (free) sandwiches.

If he saw the half full punchbowl, he couldn't resist picking it up with both hands and pouring the contents down his throat.

John MacArthur, billionaire, could never understand why he had that protruding paunch that gave him his pear shape!

◆◆◆◆◆

Does the body know when it is too fat? Research at the University of Washington Medical School in Seattle indicates that in non-fat people, the level of insulin in the cerebrospinal fluid gives the body a signal.

The researchers found that they could cause baboons to eat less and lose weight by injecting insulin directly into their brains.

The general belief is that fat people produce insulin in normal amounts, but that the brain's insulin-detecting mechanism may be faulty. Thus, obese people need higher levels of insulin to signal their bodies to say "Okay. Stop eating now!"

But alas, medical scientists haven't yet figured out how to raise the levels of insulin in the brain without causing problems in other parts of the body.

Oh well, so much for another seemingly simple solution!

Intermission

Examine your food cravings

Do you have any? Is there one very special food you have denied yourself because you feel it is a "no-no"? Select that food and once, just once, plan to have it. Plan exactly where you will sit, and when you will choose to eat it. At that time, go ahead, and fully enjoy it. See if it doesn't satisfy you. And see, too, if it hasn't short-circuited a potential eating binge.

15

Cravings: Making Them Work for You

Two chapters ago, we analyzed the food records of my friend and learned a lot about that person's likes and food involvement. You also made your own record and you examined what you consumed for three days.

What can you do to alter your lifetime eating habits? Awareness is a big first step. But what about those things you just can't live without? If they are taken away, will it be the end of the world? No. But it may feel that way right now.

We all have cravings. In order to deal with these you must do some serious analysis of your food needs.

First of all, in the words of the famed psychologist Dr. Albert Ellis, "You don't need what you want."

Read that again.

It's a deceptively simple statement. But it can apply to many things in your life. We may want many things, but how many of them are necessities?

If you learn to understand this concept you will have moved further toward conquering your overeating.

Food is an emotional issue. Some people aren't necessarily on diets, but have neurotic food attitudes. My former father-in-law had a large family and an adequate income. When the family met for a reunion and he knew he was going to take everyone to a restaurant for dinner,

he always ate at home first. Somehow he felt he was saving the money his meal would cost!

Money isn't an issue with the greedy eater. Here, it's
the belief, imagined or otherwise, that this is the last
chance he or she is ever going to have to eat the kinds of
food that are in front of them! (As if cheesecake will never
make another appearance!)

You recognize how silly this is. But you've got to learn
to believe that you can go out and buy that particular food
or something just as good anytime you crave it.

If you have between-meal hunger and simply cannot
control it, trying to attain that control may be counter-pro-
ductive—at least at this time in your life. Don't forget, we
want to set you on a positive course for the rest of your life.
That means dealing with your reality, not the reality of
some "ideal." So, if you decide you want to eat between
meals, perhaps it would be wise to think in terms of a
longer period of time to lose weight. Or, as I suggested earlier, how about trying to find out how to make those
snacks nutritious?

But what if you don't care about nutrition? What if the
only "snack" that will do the trick is a Big Mac or an ice
cream soda?

Have you thought about an ice cream soda? Are you
making a conscious decision that you want it? Are you
being impulsive? Who is in the driver's seat, you or the ice
cream soda?

If I asked myself all these questions and could honestly answer that I had made the decision to have it, I would
have the best ice cream soda I could buy. I would enjoy it
thoroughly.

Get guilt out of your life! But be aware that you will
have to pay for your snack by putting your weight goal
back somewhat. However, if the snack is important
enough, maybe it's worth the price.

You decide.

Let me give you an analogy, using a non-weight situation. A woman I knew announced to her husband that she wanted to go back to college and get her bachelor's degree. She was fifty years old at the time. Her husband said she was being silly.

"After all," he pointed out, "you'll be fifty-four years old by the time you finish."

"Well," she responded, "I'm going to be fifty-four in four more years anyway, so I may as well be fifty-four with my degree!"

You may feel that by extending your weight-loss program you will be wasting time. But don't forget, like the above scenario, time is going to pass anyway. So if you get thin a bit slower, you'll still be using the time positively.

If you tailor your new eating plan to your own lifestyle you will be successful. You will also enjoy taking control of your life. Fit that between-meal hunger into your plan and make it work for you.

You can still eat snacks and make them work for you. Let me repeat this. It is very important. Each time you decide you will eat something between meals, promise yourself that you are going to think about it. By that I mean, ask yourself "Do I really want this?" If the answer is yes, have it. But if you are less than sure, pass up the snack. Make sure you are doing the deciding, not the food.

Don't ever forget that you are the one who decided that your goal of being thinner and healthier will take a longer time to reach because you chose to eat that snack.

At this point you may decide to alter your decision. Or, perhaps not. Just keep yourself aware. And eliminate unconscious eating.

Let's return to your cravings. I understand these very well. We all have them. You don't have to be in the advanced stages of pregnancy to understand urgent food desires.

I once heard about a school teacher with a weight problem. She was at her desk when the class returned from lunch break. One of the students walked in nibbling on a donut.

After taking a few bites the students tossed it into the wastepaper basket. From the moment the remains of that donut hit the basket, the teacher could think of nothing else. When the bell rang and the class filed out at the end of the day, she dove for the donut.

Sad? Funny? A bit of both. But which of us can't identify with that story, if only in a small way?

Perhaps if the teacher had understood and accepted her cravings and fit them into her food program she wouldn't have lusted for the donut.

Why you crave certain food is complicated. It all depends on what food means to you. Is it the comfort it promises but never seems to deliver, because once you eat you suffer from guilt? Are you driven by anxiety?

For whatever reason we desire foods, it is obvious that heavy people, or even people who have their weight under control—but are food oriented—live different lives than those for whom food is merely a means to fuel the body.

Have you ever watched thin people eat? It's fascinating because it's so different from the way food-oriented people eat. For instance, a young attorney I know, for whom food is merely a means of nourishment, told me that sometimes he gets so busy at work he forgets to eat lunch.

Forgets to eat lunch!

I have been in situations where there are heated discussions going on and all I can think about is when and what I'm going to eat. Ah well, I can never be that attorney, but at least I've learned to understand and cope with my food desires.

I lost weight and have stayed thin for more than twenty-five years, but I still think about food often. And I still plan my snacks.

I'm not here to analyze you but to assist you in doing that for yourself. You do crave certain foods and if you believe you can't live without satisfying that need, you probably will be better off accepting your need rather than constantly battling against it. That way you will diffuse the explosive potential of denial.

If boredom is one of the reasons people overeat, deprivation is the major cause of diet failure.

Every time you start a new diet, you feel a sense of doom right? Isn't it because you begin with the belief that you are putting behind you all the foods you love—forever?

What I'm telling you is quite different.

You don't have to live the rest of your life without mashed potatoes. Or French fries. Or chocolate pudding. Or whatever it is you love.

I'm telling you that if you want to lose weight, and keep it off, you *must* include those favorite foods in your life. Otherwise you will feel deprived, and feelings of deprivation lead to feeling sorry for yourself.

The next step is rationalizing, and then comes the eating binge.

The most effective way to short-circuit a binge is to *plan* to have the goody you crave. When you control your food you also control the manner in which you will eat that special item. I'll show you how to make your cravings work for you rather than against you.

Is this childish?

Not at all. In fact, it's being more adult than you've been in a long time. None of us are perfect. (If you were perfect you wouldn't be reading this book.)

My craving is for the perfect chocolate chip cookie. Second best, the greatest muffins. I like sweets. I know I probably would be a few pounds lighter without them, but I have thought about how important sweets are to me and have decided that for me, they're worth having. And so I include them in my eating program. I made the decision. Nobody ever got fat from eating one chocolate chip cookie, or even one ice cream soda!

Here's how to make this work for you. First decide whether you want to include in your diet some item that you feel is worth having. Plan precisely when you will eat it and limit yourself to that single food.

Promise yourself that you will wait for the moment you set aside and keep your word to yourself. When you do this you won't nibble on lots of other things because you can wait for the time you set aside for this pleasure. And it is genuinely pleasurable.

Infants demand instant gratification. When their bellies are empty, they cry for food. But you're no longer an infant and you can get much more gratification out of planning and shaping when and where you'll indulge yourself. That, after all, is one thing that separates adults from infants.

Sometimes, I'll admit, my concentration is intense about that goody. At other times I find that I have outwitted myself. When the hour rolls around for the promised chocolate chip cookie, I find I'm too full from having eaten dinner or too sleepy, and then, I skip it

What is *your* favorite treat? French bread, chopped liver, caviar? Have it—but *you* make the decision as to when to eat it and how much.

INTERMISSSION
FOUR QUESTIONS TO ASK YOURSELF
• What was the last fad diet you went on?
• How much weight did you lose?
• How long did you keep the weight off?
• Are you ready to give up on fad diets?

16

Have You Heard This One Before?

I could have called this chapter "A Review of All the Diets of the Twentieth Century," but I like this title better. The fact is, there is very little new under the sun in dieting. Whether they call it Atkins (old or new version), Pritikin, Scarsdale, Beverly Hills, Sugar Busters, The Zone, Dean Ornish, Cabbage Soup, High Protein, Beet and Peanut Butter, Mayo Clinic, Carbohydrate Addict's Healthy Heart Program, etc., etc. just about everything has been said before.

If you think I exaggerate, let's examine the program that Dr. Atkins calls "The New Diet Revolution."

In a recent *Time* Magazine article, they referred to Atkins as the reigning guru of the low carbohydrate diets. These are diets that reduce the carbohyrates in your diet and instead suggest you eat all the protein you want. This means steak, eggs, bacon, etc. As long as you cut down on the bread, pasta, etc. you will lose weight.

Whatever they are called, *Time* Magazine continues, they are all based on this program which decreases blood-sugar levels, causing the pancreas to produce less insulin. With less insulin to draw on, the body must burn fat reserves for energy which leads to the quick weight loss.

The critics of these low-carb diets insist that by cutting out the carbs you are really reducing calories after all. You can forget about terms like ketones, (which Atkins says burn fat) and eicosanoids (which Barry Sears of *The Zone* claims are powerful hormones).

Dr. Dean Ornish (*Eat More, Weigh Less*, sort of a beyond-Pritikin approach) is appalled by carb-cutting diets. He criticizes books advising you to eat foods like bacon that won't provoke an insulin response "as if insulin is the only mechanism that affects health," and goes on to say that "Most people eat so much sugar that when they stop...they lose weight. But they're mortgaging their health in the process." Your weight loss is about achieving good health, not sacrificing it.

Unlike diet gurus like Robert Atkins, Ornish has published studies in medical journals that validate his program. He challenges the others to do the same.

Richard and Rachel Heller call themselves doctors although neither has an M.D. (They project a misleading image, wearing white coats, like hospital workers), but their *Carbohydrate Addict's Healthy Heart Program* shot to the top of the best seller lists thanks in large part to an appearance on Oprah's television show. Their plan is basically the same as Atkins with one difference. They allow one "award meal" daily wherein you can eat carbs. They are clever enough to realize, as I have been saying since the first edition of this book, that people need to have some treat—or they'll fall off their diet program.

When Dr. Robert Atkins burst onto the scene two decades ago with his "revolutionary" diet, he proposed the same high-fat, high-protein foods as he does now. The main appeal was in that magical word, "unlimited." Dr. Atkins promised that you could eat as much as you wanted of his "unlimited" foods and you would lose weight.

Your body would deliberately be put into a state of ketosis. Ketosis occurs when triglycerides (stored fat in the body) are broken down. This condition produces free fatty acids and glycerol.

Some of the free fatty acids go right to the lean body

mass to be used for fuel; the rest is partially oxidized (burned up) by the liver into "ketone bodies."

The debate continues as to whether ketosis is a harmful state for the body to be in. According to Dr. Atkins, it's wonderful. As a matter of fact, he claims ketosis is a sign "that unwanted fat is being burned up as fuel."

But...if you are a diabetic, beware, for ketosis could develop into acidosis. And if you're pregnant, ketosis could seriously threaten the fetus.

My philosophy is that anything that can harm an unborn child may be able to harm me too. However, lots of people are delighted to stop counting calories. You can indulge your desire for high-fat foods which tend to make you feel full longer.

Watch out for any diet that promises that you can eat as much as you want.

That's a misleading statement since as much as *you* want may be much more, or less, than I want. For instance, Bill Gaines, the late publisher of *Mad* magazine, thought he'd try Atkins' program. Bill loved butter, steak and heavy cream. Atkin's seemed tailor-made for him.

Telling Bill that he could eat "as much as you want" didn't take into consideration his very large capacity. He became a patient of Dr. Atkins. He gained weight. Ditto Al Goldstein. Thus Dr. Atkins' Revolution doesn't work for everyone. Like many one-sided diets, this one may work because you eat fewer calories. No matter how much you may like steak, the premise is that eventually you will grow tired, yes, even of steak, and cut down on your portions. And of course, the more unusual a diet is from what you normally eat, the more likely it is going to fail once you go back to your normal diet.

One of the more serious criticisms of this diet is that it is high in saturated fat and cholesterol. If your blood cholesterol level is high, better stay away. The danger of increasing your cholesterol is not your only concern while eating a high fat diet. Such a regime may also result in kidney and/or heart disease, vomiting or excessive uric acid in the blood which can lead to gout.

Interestingly enough, Dr. Atkins was not always a proponent of what might be called mass-medicine, since publishing a book cannot be substituted for treating people on an individual basis.

Harper's Bazaar ran an article about him the first time the Atkins diet became popular years ago. He was then a weight control consultant to one of America's great corporations. His program advocated cutting carbohydrates rather than counting calories. This was much like his later advice. One difference stressed, however, was that since carbohydrate deprivation was "as potent in weight loss as the strongest medication...*uncontrolled* [my emphasis] it is dangerous and administered haphazardly it is worthless."

Atkins spoke of this regimen's strict requirements, that it needed to be "micro-regulated, fine-tuned by the doctor in charge." In other words, in order for it to be effective it had to be done with a physician. At the time that article was published, Dr. Atkins was apparently treating obesity on a "completely individual, custom-tailored" basis.

One has to wonder when Dr. Atkins began to believe the individual treatment was not crucial and that simply following the instructions in his book would suffice. He apparently changed his opinions about fat, too.

Part of the appeal of the Atkins Diet Revolution is that it allows you all the fats you want to eat. In the early days, Dr. Atkins came out against what was then called the Air Force Diet, which encouraged the overuse of fat. That, Atkins felt, was "potentially dangerous because of its tendency to raise the serum cholesterol, thereby increasing the risk of heart disease."

In those days Atkins seemed to be diametrically opposed to the very program he later dubbed a "revolution".

But since our discussion is devoted to what is new in the field of diets, ask whether there is anything new about the Atkins Diet Revolution. The answer is no. It originated in the 19th century by a British surgeon William Harvey who, in turn, borrowed from a French doctor, Claude Bernard. The first recorded dieter using this method was William Banting who was so pleased with the weight he lost that he published *Letter on Corpulence* in 1864.

In modern times it surfaced as *Calories Don't Count* by Dr. Herman Taller. Taller prescribed soft polyunsaturated fats as a stimulus to the liver to convert fat into energy. Taller's big mistake was in promoting the sale of safflower oil along with his book—for which he was sent to prison.

It seemed he specified a specific brand of safflower oil capsules that was made by a company in which he had a large financial interest.

None of the above impresses me as much as one fact: this diet may not work. You might not lose weight. And let's not forget the possible dangers of consuming too much fat.

A variation of this diet was the High-Protein diet, like *The Doctor's Quick Weight Loss Diet* co-authored by Dr. Irwin Stillman and Samm Sinclair Baker. The information in it could fit on one side of an index card, although you probably bought the book describing it. I did too.

Essentially, you can eat as much as you want of foods that are high in protein, but this time, they must be low in fat as well. So you eat lean meats, poultry, fish, seafood, eggs and low fat cheeses. Along with the food, you must drink six to eight glasses of water each day. The water is "to wash away the ketones."

It has never been established that high-protein regimens burn calories any faster than any other diet. Moreover, according to a Harvard medical study published in the *Journal of the American Medical Association*,

too much protein can produce increases in blood cholesterol.

I tried Dr. Stillman's water diet, *The Doctor's Quick
Weight Loss Diet*. It seemed so simple. Nothing to think
about. I could eat lean chicken, fish, cottage cheese. You
are also permitted to use common seasonings such as salt,
pepper, garlic, cocktail sauce, horseradish, ketchup, herbs
and spices. There's no limit or directions on how much to
use of these items. You can imagine how creative you
become with your condiments; they soon begin replacing
the foods they are supposed to accompany.

Conclusion? The diet, if it works at all, it does so
because you are so bored, you are ready to scream at the
thought of another mouthful of anything lean.

But the water is really the topper. If you plan to try
this diet stick close to home, or plan your traveling so you
can get to a restroom frequently. I ended up dubbing this
one "Stillman's Revenge."

Stillman was a great promoter of his book and became
a familiar face on the television screen. His co-author
went to work with the late Dr. Herman Tarnower, whose
Scarsdale Diet soon had countless people carrying around
little plastic bags of spinach and dry toasted protein
bread.

The Scarsdale Diet was published in newspapers and
magazines before it became a book. This one was fully
described on one sheet of paper. Thanks to the writing
talent of Samm Sinclair Baker, one page was turned into a
book.

The regime, according to Tarnower, was "based on
chemical reactions between foods rather than quantities
of food." Simply stated, you were to use lean meat only,
prepare foods without adding fats, use lemon or vinegar
on salads and eat no substitutions! You must follow the
day-to-day food plan strictly.

According to some medical observers *The Scarsdale*

Diet was simply another low-carbohydrate, low-to-moderate-fat and high-protein diet. Although you don't count them, the calories add up to somewhere between 1,000 to 1,600 per day.

What makes *The Scarsdale Diet* effective is not eating two lamb chops on Wednesdays or cold chicken for Thursday's lunch. It works because you have reduced your intake of calories even if someone else has done the counting. That is why you are told to eat *exactly* what is assigned, with no deviation.

The Scarsdale Diet probably helped lots of people lose some weight —temporarily. But many physicians were wary. Dr. Peter Lindner, then president of the American Society of Bariatric Physicians, felt that "the effectiveness of any approach must be measured in terms of whether there will be a reduced weight in 3-5 years, rather than 3-5 weeks or even months."

The Scarsdale Diet got people to lose some weight, but what about afterward? Although the book talked about the great variety of "fine foods you may enjoy," there was also a rather extensive list of "All-Important Don'ts." These included "Don't eat candy or chocolate. Don't eat spaghetti, macaroni products, noodles, or other flour-based foods. Don't eat ice cream, ice milk, frozen custard, sherbet, or any frozen products that contain sugar or milk fats."

Never?

If *The Scarsdale Diet* was supposed to teach you how to eat for the rest of your life, I can see why people got fat again—and quickly—after they went off the program.

In order for any diet to work for you and for you to keep thin, you must understand why you eat and you must learn to handle your food needs in a way that doesn't make you feel you are depriving yourself.

Why is it important to become aware about food? Why not just go on the next fad diet and follow it down the line?

Awareness is important because once you start making your own food decisions, you won't be an easy target for every "new" diet book that hits the bookstalls.

Becoming aware means giving up your belief in fairy tales.

We are all gullible to some extent. Every fat person wants to believe that a miracle cure will appear any day now. That gullibility is too often used to manipulate fat people, through false and misleading advertisements.

Forget miracles. There are none. Only hard work and good common sense will do it. Wouldn't it be nice if my friend Wally's dream could come true? Wally always wished he could eat everything he wanted without gaining weight. "If only," he would dream, "they could insert a tube that led out from the side of my throat so I could eat and enjoy the taste of it and then just have it pass through the tube."

Sorry Wally. And sorry all the rest of you. No tubes this week.

We all think the next guy is a little weird when he comes up with an idea like that one. But weird is in the eye of the beholder. I guess the intestinal bypass operation looked weird at first. Maybe Wally's wish has been made possible by simply cutting off part of your intestines!

Before you go rushing to your surgeon for a bypass, (jejunocolostomy) understand that this is strictly a last-resort strategy. It is to be considered only after everything else has failed. And, the side effects are possible anemia, lack of calcium, and salt imbalance. Before bypass surgery, the benefits should be weighed against the possibility of other complications arising due to the bypass itself.

Clearly, it's a drastic step. Moreover, as I noted previously, there is growing evidence that bypass patients can and do regain the weight they lose.

If the bypass operation were not drastic enough, lipo-suction has become one of the most frequently performed cosmetic surgeries. I talked earlier about the surgical removal of fat. It is vacuumed right out. Thin thighs, at last. But remember, while it is true that the fat sucked from your thighs won't come back, if you do gain weight, the fat has to go somewhere—even if it's not your thighs. Some people find fat appearing in places they never had it before—the backs of their arms, in the stomach, etc.

Shall we continue with more of the bizarre methods?

Some years ago there was a popular machine called the Relaxicizor. The impression was given that electrical current running from the machine to your body made the muscles contract and ultimately firm up.

One federal judge, upon hearing testimony on it, decided it might cause heart failure as well as possibly exacerbate "epilepsy, hernia, multiple sclerosis, spinal fusion, tuboovarian abscess, ulcers and varicose veins." Well, anyway, the Federal Drug Administration put the Relaxicizor on the prescription list.

I recalled what I'd read about the Relaxicizor when I found an article in *Us* magazine about the Biobody Machine. This machine was discovered by Sasha and Hoanna Muniak during their honeymoon in Hong Kong. The machine was used in Japan on hospital patients for muscle therapy. The Muniaks now use it in their Biobody Center to stimulate muscle contraction. The article suggests further that "a 35- minute session aimed at specific trouble spots, such as the abdominal area, can equal 1500 sit-ups."

Hmmm. Has the Relaxicizor been reincarnated?

No concept is too farfetched for someone, somewhere, who is desperately reaching for relief from the fat syndrome. That is why educating yourself about the realities of various reducing programs is important. If you learn the validity of the programs, you'll be able to make your own, intelligent decision.

Anything magical, avoid. All magic is illusion, no matter how well-performed. You want to achieve a long-term weight loss and a way of eating for the rest of your life, not one that will encourage pounds to reappear like the rabbit in a magician's hat.

Magic always makes me think of hypnosis. Many people have tried that too. For some, it has been known to help for a while. But since you aren't learning anything about how to eat, or why you eat, once the hypnotic suggestions wears off, you know by now what happens.

Not long ago an approach was introduced using the principle of acupuncture. In this instance, a special type of staple was permanently implanted in the patient's ear. Whenever unwanted eating seemed imminent all one had to do was stimulate the staple in a certain way and that activated nerve impulses which ended the desire to eat.

Sounds good. It was unsuccessful for an interesting reason. In order to make it work, the person had to stimulate the staple, and in many cases they just didn't do that. You see, nothing—even the most foolproof method—will work all the time. You must want it to work.

Remember cellulite? If you are female you probably have heard of and, Lord knows, feared cellulite. Cellulite, we were led to believe, is fatty tissue deposited in certain areas of the body—specifically the thighs, but also often on the upper arm.

There really is no such thing as cellulite according to Dr. Willibald E. Nagler, Physiatrist-in-chief of New York Hospital at Cornell Medical Center. The word, taken from the French meaning "leather reinforcement on riding breeches," is "meaningless." Dr. Nagler says that the only way to get rid of this fat is by reducing caloric intake and by doing a great deal of aerobic exercise (swimming, jogging running, bicycling, jumping rope, walking—briskly).

Best of all, keep your weight down and your muscles strong and you may not get it at all.

If it were only possible to reduce where we would like! Dr. Donald S. Robertson of Scottsdale, Arizona, says, "I always explain to patients that we do not have much control over exactly where body fat will be lost, and that many times in order to get rid of abnormal thigh and abdominal deposits of fat [read: cellulite], we sometimes have to lose more total body fat than is desired, and the face and arms may become wrinkled in this process, but the undesirable fat will also ultimately disappear."

Apparently one way to get rid of "cellulite" is to diet enough to lose those fatty deposits. "Cellulite" is simply fatty tissue, no different from any other fatty tissue. Don't fall prey to the gadgets advertised that lead you to believe fat can be scrubbed away.

Whether you have contemplated bypass surgery or have merely been irked by the presence of "cellulite" on your body, you are not alone. Many hundreds of thousands of people have been ripe for the misleading promises of instant thinness.

None of these methods are solutions to your weight problem. You have the solution, and are now acquiring necessary knowledge about what works and what does not. And you are now ready to accept responsibility for your own weight.

Once you accept responsibility for making yourself fat, you can take responsibility for making yourself thin, too. The nice part of that is you can take all the credit for your success. You don't have to thank Dr. Stillman, Dr. Atkins, or any other doctor or quack diet you read about.

Weight control does involve giving up some infantile behavior. The rewards are more than worth it, believe me.

I know it is not easy to give up on miracles. A man I interviewed is probably the perfect example of the kind of person who will spend twice as much time and money looking for magical solutions than it would take if he just tried to lose weight sensibly.

A few years ago he was desperate. He learned of a "new" diet. It entailed daily visits to a physician's office where he was injected with something called HCG or Human Chronic Gonadotrophin. This is derived from the urine of pregnant women. The regimen was described by A.T.W. Simeons, M.D., in *Pounds and Inches: A New Approach to Obesity* published in 1972 in Italy. Dr.Simeons claimed that "the injection of only 125 units per day [of HCG] is ample to reduce weight at the rate of roughly one pound per day, even in a colossus weighing 400 pounds, when associated with a 500-Calorie diet."

Okay. So this fellow showed up every day at the doctor's office, dropped his trousers and bent over for his shot. The nurse (he rarely saw the doctor after the initial visit) handed him his food for the rest of the day.

At the end of the prescribed period of time he had lost a great deal of weight. It also cost him a lot of money. (Pregnant women's urine does not come cheap!)

He never once considered that anyone limiting himself to 500 calories a day would lose weight, with or without the injection.

Dr. Simeons talked about how long the treatment should last. "Patients who need to lose 15 pounds (7 kg.) or less require 26 days treatment with 23 daily injections. The extra three days are needed because all patients must continue the 500-Calorie diet for three days after the last injection. This is a very essential part of the treatment, because if they start eating normally as long as there is even a trace of HCG in their body they put on weight alarmingly at the end of the treatment."

There is no way you can eat only 500 calories a day for twenty-six days and *not* lose weight.

But all the people who paid their money and dropped their pants didn't want to hear that. They were looking for the miracle. And even if they hated getting those shots, they held still for them.

I wonder how many kept their weight down. I know this man did not. Once he was on his own again and had no shots in the buttocks and no nurse handing him food, he had to make selections. And he was back to square one again.

Interestingly, I read recently that Janet Jackson is involved in pretty much the same regime that I just described.

Fact: Any "crash" diet can result in weight loss. The rest of it is the stuff dreams are made of. And remember my philosophy: A so-called diet has a beginning and an ending.

What I advocate is a new lifetime approach to eating. There is no ending date. You change your approach to food forever.

That's why it works.

That's why it worked for me.

As Gilbert Leveille, Chairman of the Department of Food Science and Human Nutrition of Michigan State University, expressed it, "You can lose weight on just about any diet if you stick to it, but a fad or crash dieter will tend to stop and start diets often in the course of a year or two and ultimately gain five or ten pounds."

Did you read those last six words? Do you recognize yourself somewhere in that statement? What is there about us foodaholics that wants to believe in every fad, even though we know, somewhere within us, that there is no real miracle diet? Unless we learn to change the way we eat, we will lose and then gain again. No fooling.

Ah, but hope springs eternal.

I guess the ultimate dream is fake fat. Technically called sucrose polyester (SPE) this is supposed to help reduce and lower blood cholesterol.

SPE was synthesized by Fred H. Mattson, Ph.D., while he was a research scientist at Proctor & Gamble. SPE is supposed to imitate food fats in texture and taste, but—it is not broken down by the intestine and not absorbed by the body. Now on the market as such brand name products as Olestra, SPE is calorie-free. It "binds cholesterol on its way through the intestines and carries it out in the feces. The result? Your serum cholesterol level can be brought down."

It hasn't been the overwhelming success that had been anticipated. Why? Maybe it has something to do with the fact that sometimes it results in upset stomachs and even anal leakage. Oops. Definitely not a pretty thought.

But why look for fake fat? Isn't it better to learn to live with less real fat?

There is genuine research going on in bariatrics, and one discovery is leptin. This molecule acts on the brain as a kind of natural weight control system. In a study done with mice, it was reported that leptin made genetically fat mice stop eating and become thin. When this hormone was found in people it was hoped that obesity might be a simple matter of leptin deficiency. But as it stands, overweight people produce lots of leptin. As a matter of fact, scientists could only find a half-dozen people in the world who don't make leptin. One, a 3-year-old girl, ate 2000 calories at a sitting. When treated with leptin these people do lose weight.

Leptin is thought to act in the brain, telling it that you are in danger from food restriction since starvation is actually more of a threat to survival than obesity. Perhaps one day leptin may, indeed, lead to a great advance in the treatment of obesity. For the time being, however, we'll have to settle on realistic food choices and behavioral changes.

Intermission

Have you ever had a "good friend" encourage you to eat when you knew it was the wrong thing to do?

Make a list of those of your family, friends and acquaintances who try to push food at you. This is your secret "enemies list." Henceforth, you must be constantly on guard when you and anyone on the list and food are all in the same place.

17

Sabotage

o you know what I'm talking about when I refer to
when I mention the enemy? I touched on this earlier when I told you about my sister, Jane. Jane,
who was chronically overweight, had a husband who
seemed determined to keep her that way. Any time she
had to lose weight, he felt threatened that he might lose
her, and so he did everything he could do to sabotage her
weight loss plans.

This is not unusual. As a matter of fact, it is more com-
monplace than many of us know. When people who try
to reduce share their experiences with others, one hears
the frequent complaint that those people who say they
want to help us, really work against us.

The most obvious situation is that of parents who
believe they are being thoughtful when they urge the child
to eat that special dessert "only this once." At times like
these, the dieter is frequently made to feel guilty for not
eating.

I'm sure you have all heard things like "But I spent all
day cooking this, and now you're not even going to taste
it?" All too often cleaning your plate is interpreted as giving love to the person feeding you.

How many of us have eaten foods to avoid hurting
other people's feelings? Plenty.

These feeding-friends are misguided. A true friend is

one who encourages you in your effort, not one who complicates your problem.

In an article published in *Obesity/Bariatric Medicine*, a case was described where a patient had managed to maintain a 75-pound weight loss for a year and a half. Ironically, since the weight had come off, his family and friends greet him with: "Have you gained any weight yet?" I don't have to tell you that this is not the most helpful question to ask someone trying to stay thin.

First, the patient had to reassure himself that it was *their* problem, not his. He wasn't giving any cues to provoke this question. He also realized that he shouldn't respond emotionally to what others think, say or do about this dieting.

It's very difficult when you seek encouragement, and don't get any, to hold on to your new thin image. Analyze why people say the things they do. For one thing, don't dismiss the "sour grapes" that so-called friends sometimes have.

It's like the old saying, "I want my friends to do well, but not so well that they do better than I."

It would be lovely to live in a perfect world, where everyone responds to us just as we would like, but if the world were perfect, we probably would not have the weight to lose in the first place.

A woman I know who lost a great deal of weight found herself reevaluating many friendships, especially those of her "friends" who had cautioned her against losing "too much weight."

It's sad, but a friend who is jealous of your success in getting thin and more attractive isn't a friend at all. That is a person who needs to feel superior to the people around him or her in order to feel adequate. Phase such people out of your life and seek new relationships.

Ironically, losing a great deal of weight is very much like becoming a new person.

If you realize that other people are not accustomed to dealing with you in your changed form, you can better understand that they need to adjust to this metamorphosis, just as you do. This doesn't excuse their counterproductive gestures, but might give *you* insight into possible motivation for such actions.

It's difficult to imagine people sabotaging your efforts, when it should be obvious to them how important their help is to your success. However, human interaction is quite complicated.

In *People Around You Can Make You Fat* Lee Headley, Ph.D., described a man who had weighed 490 pounds and lost 238 of them. At the time I read this he was trying desperately to put the weight back on. Why? It seems his wife, for whom he was trying to improve his figure, left him, complaining that since dieting he had lost his sense of humor.

You and I might ask, "Who needs a companion like that?" Obviously, to this fellow, she was more important to please than himself. He chose to blame himself as being awful to live with and soon felt he was "getting back to my old self now."

If that's true love, save me from it!

Tell your friends, loved ones and relatives: "If you really love me, don't feed me." But at the same time, remember, just as it was you who put the weight on, and you who are taking it off, it's your task to deal with this problem too.

(I don't know of a single case where someone put a loaded pistol to an overweight person's head and said, "Eat!")

Beware of feeders. Gently but firmly refuse their "kind offers" of food "just this once," if you have decided it's against your better interest. This is difficult, I know, and you will sometimes find yourself jeopardizing relationships. However, you must consider how thoughtless the other person is being in not considering you.

You can devise all sorts of methods to dissuade your friends from over-feeding you. Some people like to see everybody at a party with a drink. Don't fight it. Just hold a glass of club soda with a slice of lemon or lime and you'll blend in with the crowd.

At a dinner party, make sure you leave some food on your plate. Otherwise, they'll be eager to rush in with seconds. Or, when being pressed to "Just take a taste," tell them you have an allergy to that food. You'll find that no one ever tries to feed you food that might bring on a rash!

Don't be afraid to be an eccentric. If you find yourself overwhelmed with a tempting array of foods, and don't want to blow your diet, announce loud and clear, "Oh golly, too bad. Today is the day I always fast." That way, everyone will be watching to see if you break down. It will make you even more determined to stick with your resolve.

Beware, too, of "friends" who tell you how drawn and sickly you look after you have dropped some weight.

After Lyle Stuart had lost more than 80 pounds many people greeted him by telling him he looked awful. When a fat person loses weight his formerly round features become more slender.

Many people not only told him how terrible he looked, but that he looked better fat!

If you are involved in a program such as Weight Watchers or Overeaters Anonymous, these groups can be particularly helpful at times when you feel acquaintances are trying to sabotage your efforts. As I mentioned earlier, it is the support system that such groups rely upon that make the dieter feel understood and motivated.

You may be thinking that you have problems enough trying to reduce. Who needs to add to these by having to understand the motivations of others? If you look upon this knowledge as a vehicle that ultimately works for your well-being, perhaps it's easier to accept.

If you understand what motivates these saboteurs you will be more secure in what you are trying to accomplish. Moreover, you will begin to accept your own judgment of yourself rather that those of others.

Just because someone tells you that the weight you lost makes your wrinkles stand out more, or that you looked better fat, doesn't make it true.

There are instances when people may genuinely be puzzled and even disturbed by your weight loss. Young children sometimes feel threatened by any change in a parent. Don't forget, to that child you are not fat, you are Mommy or Daddy. And children think you are perfect just the way you are.

Moreover, children see the entire world as centered around them. Thus, your weight loss may make them worry about losing part of you, or worrying about other things in their world changing.

In *The Psychologist's Eat-Anything Diet,* Dr. Leonard Pearson described one youngster who said, "You're not fat, Mommy. You're soft. Don't you change."

As Dr. Pearson advises, reassure your children. Point out that their bodies keep changing but that doesn't alter the family loving one another. Assure the child, too, that you will love yourself better when you are thin.

As children approach adolescence and beyond, an obese parent can turn from "perfection" into a source of extreme embarrassment to that same child. Don't be surprised to hear demands to "get thin, please!" from your kids. They love you, all right, but will be more comfortable if you don't stand out in a crowd because of your fat.

Which brings me to an important question: Will *you* love yourself better when you are thin? Don't answer right away, because the answer may not be the obvious one.

In order to really love yourself better thin you should first find out what it is that made you fat. Deep in your heart, do you dislike yourself? Are you punishing yourself with your fatness? Or, are you building an armor against the world of disappointments and frustrations?

INTERMISSION

Why do you eat excessively?

Take a pencil and check the reasons below that apply to you. Then, number the #1, #2, #3 etc., in the order in which they start you overeating.

( ) Boredom   #_____
( ) Anxiety   #_____
( ) Anger   #_____
( ) Loneliness   #_____
( ) Depression   #_____
( ) Frustration   #_____
( ) Sexual frustration#_____
( ) Fear: specific   #_____
( ) Fear: nameless   #_____
( ) Love of food   #_____
( ) Sugar syndrome #_____

18
Why Do We Eat?

Hungry?
Bored?
Anxious?
Angry?
Afraid?
Depressed?

Y ou can add to the list, I'm sure. How often, though, do you ask yourself, "Why am I putting this into my mouth?" Singer Carnie Wilson recently told a television interviewer it was because she didn't feel love from her dad. She lost 44 pounds by drinking more water and cutting out snacks. Ultimately, however, she gained the weight back and recently had a radical surgical procedure performed which anyone interested could watch on the Internet. This, she hopes, will help her to keep the weight off.

I know I eat for all of the above reasons. And more. I eat when I'm frustrated. I eat when I don't want to get to the work that I know I must get done. As I write this book I find myself wanting to jump up and raid the refrigerator. Eating is a great way to avoid getting down to business.

I suppose the only time I *don't* think of eating is when I'm having sex, exercising or taking a tango lesson. But why do you and I eat under these circumstances—while someone else does not? I'm not going to psychoanalyze you. I'd like to help open the door to discovery. What is it that drives you into self-destructive eating? Once the door to self-understanding is open, it will be up to you to close it when you wish.

I told you in the beginning that I was never the heaviest person alive nor am I now the thinnest. But I have struggled with weight most of my life and I understand how difficult it is not only to lose weight but to keep it off.

I consider getting thin an enormous effort. It's one I've gone through many times. And it takes so much energy that I never again want to get fat enough to face what I call a "real" diet—one that will take more than a day or two, or maybe three, to take off the pounds that creep back.

It used to be difficult for me to understand how people could lose 50, 60, 100 and even more pounds, and then gain them all back again. I wanted to shake them by the shoulders and tell them, "Dummy! Wasn't it torture enough to take off those pounds? Can't you see that you're getting fat again?"

Of course I was not aware then of the many and varied reasons people eat.

One reason people reduce and then get fat again is because they are honestly afraid to be thin. No, don't laugh. What will it mean to be thin?

For one thing, they won't be able to hide behind their fat any longer. They will be just like everybody else. They won't be able to wallow in self-pity and blame other people for making them fat. And they will also have to face life's failures and disappointments without having fat as an excuse. Forced to stand on their own, taking responsibility for their own actions—growing up.

That *is* scary!

It has been observed that psychological disorders suffered by the obese are more likely to be caused by being overweight than they are causes for the overweight.

Don't think, though, that fat people are more likely to

be neurotic. Dr. Albert Stunkard, a psychiatrist at the University of Pennsylvania found in a study of New Yorkers, "only a 'trivial' difference between normal-weight and obese people in the amount and degree of mental illness."

But normal weight people don't have the added problem that fat ones do after reducing. Dr. Jules Hirsch of Rockefeller University in New York observed that "when obese people lose a lot of weight, a large percentage of them become depressed and anxious...Many such people feel 'deprived, left out, lonesome and empty in a global sense.'"

Does this ring a bell for you? If so, it's particularly important to learn about how *you* deal with food. If you don't understand the interaction between yourself and the food you will certainly continue to ride the roller coaster of getting thin and getting fat again. I want you to break that pattern once and forever. You can, you know. It's within *your* control.

Have you ever observed how overweight people just can't seem to throw food away? They'll go out and buy their food, eat to their satisfaction, and then, unable to discard it but not wanting to eat more, will offer it to a neighbor. A friend of mine is the neighbor of a magazine publisher who is forever on a diet. She's getting fat on his leftovers.

Do you have the fantasy that if only you can get thin, all aspects of your life will change? Will all your problems disappear?

No, and you knew that. While it is true that you will change—drastically—the change in the physical you does not automatically mean that all other facets of your personality will change too. You have to work on changing them, if that's your desire.

Weight-related problems may end once you are thin, but don't be staggered to discover that you still have trouble getting the kids off to school on time, or that the house still needs dusting. The fantasy fades for fantasy-lovers. To soothe themselves they begin to nibble again. And up, up, up goes the dial on the scale.

Gloria, a woman I interviewed for this book, lost more than seventy pounds after being overweight all of her life. Her goal was, at long last, within her grasp. Only twenty more pounds. She already looked great, although the additional twenty pounds would obviously make her a knockout. She began to falter as she approached her goal.

When she questioned herself, she realized that deep in her heart she was afraid to be thin. Part of the reason was that throughout fat adulthood, people—even strangers—would stop her on the street or on an elevator and make remarks such as, "If you ever lose weight, life will be yours," and "You'll have men dropping at your feet."

What happened as she got thinner? Neither of those things. In fact, life was pretty much as it always had been. Naturally, she was disappointed. Was it all worth it?

She had not prepared herself for anything less than a total revolution in her life. But the reality is that lots of people are thin. So what? Men don't fall at your feet just because you are of normal weight. You have to find some other means of attracting attention. You must compete on the same terms as everyone else. If you don't understand this, losing weight *can* be a big letdown.

It's as if you have been working on something and when you are ready to unveil it, the world looks at you, slightly puzzled. Unless you discover why you eat and are clear in your own mind about why you are losing weight, you may put it all back on.

But self-knowledge and self-understanding can become barricades against doing it again. Knowing what it is that makes *you* put on weight, again and again, can finally work to keep it off.

When you lose weight to please yourself, you get your

own positive feedback. You will like yourself better thin and won't need to depend on the reactions of outsiders.

Some fat people get a great deal of consolation from eating. If they are lonely or unhappy or under stress, out comes the dish of crackers and cheese.

According to Dr. Lee Headley in *People Around You Can Make You Fat*, the funeral feast probably was born of a desire to soothe discomfort and grief. At funerals many faiths share food, which provides comfort and a shared expression of pain and sorrow.

Food does comfort. Don't let anyone tell you otherwise. Sure, it keeps us alive, but we've come a long way since eating served primarily as a tool for survival. That's how it is in our Western civilization.

Wandering in the aisles of a supermarket or driving past the fast food restaurants that polka dot our major highways makes it difficult to realize there is still starvation in many parts of the world.

Food was the first comforting factor in our infant lives, as our mothers nourished us. But the way overweight people use food for comfort is what sets them apart from others.

Fat people use food as a way of rewarding themselves. Although most heavy people think of having no control over themselves when they eat too much, in reality they actually are controlling the forces that bother them by feeding themselves.

Food as reward for getting a lousy job done, a consolation for feeling unhappy, for getting the grass cut—all these are neurotic uses of food.

Have you ever seen a trainer reward a chimpanzee for performing his task in a circus? Put yourself in the chimp's place—maybe it will shock you into realizing what you are doing with food.

Food can be a pleasure; it should be. But you are not a performing animal. If a chimpanzee were more intelligent he might not accept a food reward; he might demand instead a trip to Paris. You have the option of feeding yourself because you have completed a task, or using some other, more constructive reward.

How about shopping? I hate to admit it, because shopping is such stereotypical behavior for women. But I'm going to let you in on something I discovered about myself not too long ago. When I feel down, shopping gives me a lift. Good or bad, it's the truth. And I'll tell you something else, it's not fattening!

When I buy something to wear and it looks good on me, it helps to keep me from eating. The reason isn't very complicated. It's because it pleases me to see myself in the new skirt, or sweater, etc., and I know if I get heavy, it just won't look good.

But it isn't only shopping for clothes that gives me that lift. I can get some of the same good feelings shopping for greeting cards, stationery, or a beautiful coffee mug. You get the idea. The point is, instead of being "good" to myself with food, I have found other ways to please myself.

Try to substitute some pleasurable experience in place of your food rewards. Do you like to play golf? The next time you feel you have completed a particularly arduous task, go to a golf course or tennis court and enjoy. Or sign up for a dance class or French lessons.

How about giving yourself an hour in a sauna and a massage?

Indulge your pleasure-oriented fantasies. You'll find that you feel fulfilled even more than you were when you hid in your room and ate a bag of jelly donuts. Or if money is scarce, run a tub of warm water and luxuriate in some Ivory liquid.

Many people eat because they are angry. They are angry and cannot express that anger directly. How many times have you fought with your husband (or wife) or your kids or your parents and then found yourself in the kitchen?

Sometimes eating is an expression of both anger and control. Certainly, it's a distorted sense of control. But control all the same.

Wouldn't it be better to let off that steam where you know it belongs? Get angry aloud. Tell the kids off. Are you afraid people won't like you because you yell occasionally? Bottling up anger can lead not only to food binges, but to more and more suppressed feelings of rage. Picture a pot ready to boil over and you'll know what I mean. If you take the lid off, you diffuse the anger and you can deal with it appropriately.

First, accept the idea that it's okay to be angry sometimes. Everybody gets mad. And those who express their anger don't go around on the brink of a real blowup. They are less likely to develop ulcers too!

If you eat when you are angry, who ends up being hurt by your rage? You do, of course. Feeding yourself when you're angry isn't going to make you feel better. It isn't even going to console you. It may make you fatter. And that surely isn't going to lessen your anger, is it?

I'm aware that this may make perfect sense on paper, but the next time you come home from work and find Tom hasn't walked the dog, or done his homework, and the garbage is piled up because no one took it out—you may still find yourself eating instead of giving Tommy hell.

Try—just once—to handle your anger differently.

By the way, are you aware that obese people are rarely seen overeating? I mean, you don't see them actually putting food in their mouths. I know that my sister, Jane, almost never finished the food on her plate.

I questioned others who had struggled with weight problems to see if this was unique. One man told me that after a lifetime of sitting at his family's table and being criticized for taking an extra piece of bread or a second help-ing, after hearing over and over, "Do you really need that?" he finally withdrew from eating publicly. He would wait until he was alone and could satisfy his eating needs in peace.

For others, eating is an act of defiance. It is saying to those who constantly hammer away at you: "My eating is one thing you can't control!" But of course, who suffers but you?

I've been straight with you all the way so let me tell you something nobody talks about. You've heard of "will power." And when you don't stay with your regimen, you chastise yourself for lack of "will power".

Where is that "will power" supposed to come from? Some mysterious place deep within you?

Applesauce.

You can't buy "will power" at Bloomingdale's or Nordstrom's. It doesn't grow in a rose garden. It doesn't rain from heaven. The fact is, it is like the Emperor's new clothes. It doesn't exist, except in our imaginations.

So-called will power has to be self-generated. It has to come from inside. And the problem is that the will power oil drill may work twenty-three and a half hours a day but there will come that time when you reach in for the will power and the pump is dry.

I've been much more successful with "won't power." Yes, won't power!

I won't eat those chocolate cupcakes because I'm going to trade them off for the pleasure of feeling better and looking better. I'd love to eat those chocolate cup-cakes, but I know from experience that I won't like myself or feel particularly good if I eat them. So I'll trade off immediate pleasure for pleasure to come.

It's like the things people do with money. Some of us can't hold on to it. We spend for immediate pleasure. The result is often deep insecurity because we have no funds to fall back on. Contrast this with the person who allows for some pleasure, but also makes a regular bank deposit.

Passing by things you'd like to eat with "won't power" is like putting money in the bank. You'll get all that pleasure to come—and with interest.

Changing eating habits isn't easy. For some people, it seems no matter how much they eat or don't eat, they stay fat or get fatter. My good friend Phyllis virtually has to stop eating in order to lose any weight. And even then it comes off in meager ounces while she hungers to lose pounds.

For those of us who used to think that "eat less, lose weight" was gospel, I don't know if it comes as good news or bad news to learn that it often is harder for fat people to reduce than it is for those just looking to drop a couple of pounds.

Dr. Judith Rodin, a psychologist at Yale University, points out that "fat people produce higher levels of insulin, a hormone that promotes storage of calories as fat. High levels of insulin also cause hunger and result in increased food consumption. The faster a person eats and the more calories and carbohydrates the meal contains, the more insulin is released creating a cycle of more eating and more insulin." Translated into plain language: fat people have bodies that are out of sync, and eat more because their bodies cause them to.

To make matters worse, according to Dr. Jules Hirsch of Rockefeller University in New York, pound for pound, overweight people "need a third to a half fewer calories to maintain their weight than people of normal weight."

Ye Gads! That makes you want to throw the towel in, doesn't it? What's the point in trying? It seems as though there's just no way to succeed.

Not true. I cite these grim facts, not to discourage you, but to let you know that if you are suffering, it's probably with good reason. Once you understand that it is harder for you to lose weight than other people you will be reassured that you weren't going crazy after adding up your daily caloric intake and finding it came to 500 but you still hadn't lost any weight yet!

Knowledge is an important tool. Ignorance can only breed frustration and overeating.

Let's finish with the depressing part of the scenario.

Not long ago scientists investigated the phenomenon I've just described. Dr. John H. Karam, director of the Metabolic Research Unit of the University of California at San Francisco, found that fat people either have a normal number of fat cells which have become enlarged because they eat more calories than are used up, or they have too many fat cells and these, too, are enlarged.

I mentioned earlier that the number of fat cells a person has is determined during childhood. It is therefore terribly important to not overfeed children, since infancy and adolescence are two periods in a person's life when the greatest amount of growth occurs. (I am not ignoring liposuction, which does remove fat cells permanently. However, if you recall, you still can gain weight. Even though you won't replace those removed fat cells, you will put weight on elsewhere. Often where you least want it.)

But what about those of us to whom this information comes a number of years too late?

Despair is nonproductive. Learn to be realistic about your weight goals and about how long it may take you to reach them. Understand your particular limitations. Before we part, I will help you to design a reducing program that will no longer frustrate you.

Brighten up! My approach is one you can embrace with no reservations because it will be one with attainable goals.

Do you have a morbid curiosity about discovering whether you are one of the "unlucky" ones? A physician can determine if you have high blood levels of insulin, triglycerides, and glucose, which could indicate that your fat cells are too big. If losing weight brings the three levels to normal, chances are the fat cells are down to normal size too.

Finding out isn't going to make you thin. But it need not diminish your determination to get thin. You may not be able to control the number of fat cells but you can control the size of them. If you are overweight and your blood levels are normal for insulin, triglycerides and glucose, it suggests that your fat cells are of normal size—even though they are too numerous.

Again, the focus here should be on reducing the stress connected with trying to get thin. *Don't allow yourself to get discouraged because it's slow going for you* .

I know how alone you feel when you start a new diet. But you couldn't be less alone. It has been estimated that some fifty million Americans have serious weight problems. No, this information won't make you feel better; but at least you'll know that being overweight is not the loneliest game in town.

In the next chapters we're going to examine some of the commonly held myths about being fat.

Myths About Dieting and Eating

We all cling to certain excuses for why we are overweight. Probably the most common one is "I have a sluggish metabolism and so no matter how I try, I can't lose weight."

Watch out, Pinocchio, your nose is starting to grow!

Well, maybe that's not entirely fair. Maybe you really believe your statement. But more than likely it isn't true. It is true that whereas most fat people start out metabolically normal, as they gain weight, research (done by Dr. Jerome Knittle of Mount Sinai Medical Center in New York, among others) shows that they may "gradually develop derangements in their internal chemistry." And, as these people often complain, this chemical derangement "can cause 'everything' they eat to turn to fat and result in weight gain even though they do not seem to overeat."

Another widely held myth is that fat people eat because they are emotionally disturbed. I've already quoted authorities who have concluded psychological disorders are more likely the *results* than the cause of obesity.

And if you think you are fat because you inherited the "tendency," I offer myself as an example that it is not necessary to fulfill that destiny. For those of us with such inherited tendencies, obesity should be thought of as just that—a tendency; one you can never forget, but one that can be controlled.

True, there are instances where physical problems are a very real part of the problem. If you have certain chronic conditions which require medical attention, these must always be taken into consideration before and during any weight-loss program.

Obviously, if you suffer from high blood pressure, arthritis, diabetes, or other special problems, you must work with a physician in selecting a program that will help you lose weight without putting your health in jeopardy.

But don't use a health condition to get off the hook, either. Obesity itself is a major factor in reducing your life span by leading to serious illnesses such as stroke, heart attack, and diabetes. To put it bluntly, there is nothing bad that will happen to you if you reduce and bring your weight down to normal.

As for diabetes, the Pritikin Program makes a persuasive case for losing weight. By simply reducing, eating properly and exercising regularly, most people can bring insulin levels down to a satisfactory level and get diabetes under control.

It's critical to remember, if you have a special health problem, never, never go on a diet until you consult a physician.

Incidentally, obesity is not restricted to humans. Many people jokingly point out that after an extended period of time of living together, people often begin to look like their pets. An English study observed that "the pets of fat people are twice as likely to be fat as the pets of thin people."

That may sound funny, but if you have a dog like mine, it can be a real problem. Tara is my tiny toy poodle, weight about seven pounds. As I sit and nibble my cookie and sip my tea I find myself giving her the crumbs. It doesn't take very much overeating to make a seven pound dog fat!

Have you ever wondered if fat people are inactive

because of their weight or as a result of it? It gets hard to separate the chicken from the egg, doesn't it?

We've talked about exercise as an aid to weight loss. Let's talk about it for another minute. If you are very much overweight I doubt that you are the sort of person who would seriously embark on a vigorous workout program. Nor would it probably appeal to you to take up skiing or paddle ball, although you can burn up many calories doing those activities.

The fact is, you might just kill yourself too.

Once again, I recommend walking. Not only can you walk at any age, but it will tax your body far less for long periods of time than any other form of exercise.

Go for a walk. Take the dog for a walk. It will help the dog, too. Don't have a dog? Buy one. Or jog over to your local Humane Society and get one, free.

We haven't yet touched on the effect of overweight on your sex life. On the most practical level, if you're extremely heavy you obviously limit your sexual flexibility. However, on an emotional level, I have spoken to fat people who confide that they are embarrassed by their bodies and tend to shy away from sexual contact.

In one such instance described in *The Psychology of Successful Weight Control* by Mary Catherine Tyson, M.D., and Robert Tyson, Ph.D., one young woman was advised by her doctor to lose weight. She knew losing would make her healthy and certainly improve her social life. However, she continued to eat as much as before and even gained weight.

When she discussed this problem with the physician, she admitted the fear of attracting men. She had been raised by strict parents and was taught that sex was distasteful. Her lesson was so well learned that she unconsciously avoided men by making herself physically unattractive. Thus, in her case, staying fat meant staying "safe."

Yet, in other cases, obese women may become sexually aggressive because, fully aware of their appearance, they have decided not to be overlooked by men. Instead, they are the active pursuers of partners. Many, however, choose men who are sexually submissive, and who ultimately do not fulfill them.

As far as sexuality goes, though, fat people are just as interested in sex as the next person. Don't delude yourself by believing otherwise. But it also may be true that your sex drive can decrease because the added bulk you're carrying makes it more difficult to get around.

I hope it's clear that we are not eliminating either gender from this discussion. Men and women can be equally sensitive because of their body weight and can have sexual hang-ups.

During the period of life when men are passing through their climacteric (male menopause) they experience symptoms which are similar to those women encounter at menopause. Because hormonal changes are occurring, some men gain weight. With the weight gain they may feel their sexual powers leaving them. It's important for them to understand that sexual powers are decreasing not because of the "change of life" but rather, because they are getting heavy.

As our aging population grows, we are learning that the sex drive continues well into our golden years. If you're fat, that may be why you're not sexually driven. Age probably has little to do with it.

In *You Can Be Fat-Free Forever*, Doctors L. Melvin Elting and Seymour Isenberg describe one man who was having such an experience. After becoming thinner than he had been in thirty years, he found himself comfortably passing through the male menopause and emerging more sexually active than before. As he put it, "I've discovered there's a lot more still left for me in life than food."

There are many commonly believed myths about

weight. Over years of research, I've accumulated a file of ideas about why people do and do not lose weight. I won't cite them all, but it's worthwhile taking a quick look at a few.

◆◆◆◆◆

If you stay on your diet you will lose weight every week. The fact is, we all reach plateaus where no weight loss occurs. If you believe you *must* lose weekly pounds, it will throw you off course.

After dieting for a while, the stomach shrinks. (This is one I always thought was true.) The fact is, if you reduce the quantity of food you eat, after your weight is down for several months you will actually feel full sooner because you require less food. It's a matter of getting your body accustomed to the smaller quantities. Your stomach does not change size.

When I was much heavier, I can recall going with friends for our usual Sunday night Chinese dinner. There were four of us, and we always ordered food enough for six. I think we believed we would have leftovers to take home, but there seldom were. As I lost weight I found myself amazed at how my capacity dwindled. I just could not consume the same quantity of food as I did earlier. Had my stomach shrunk? I thought so, until I learned the above.

I like to think that my body has outsmarted me. I put it that way because when I was reducing I would plan that when I got thin, I would always save room for dessert at dinner, no matter what. I'm a person who scans the dessert section of a menu first, and then decides my other courses. Thus, if I see a tempting dessert I adjust my dinner to accommodate it.

Ironically, I often find myself too full to eat the dessert. Yes, *too full*. I never dreamed that could happen on my way down, but it has. I'll bet you don't think that will ever happen to you, either.

It will.

You need extra vitamins while you are dieting. We certainly are hammered at by television and radio as well as print ads to make us believe so. But if you eat a well-balanced diet, there is no need for vitamin supplements. Moreover, if you think you can go on a fad diet and supplement what your body is lacking by taking vitamins, that isn't going to happen either.

I heard the strangest example of this attitude from a man who called in to one of those radio call-in talk shows. This day the studio guest was a diet specialist who was also an expert in nutrition.

The caller had a problem. He had devised a fad diet of his own. He ate dry cereal which came in single portion boxes. He did this because he could read the ingredients listed on the side of the box and know exactly how many calories he was consuming. It also gave the vitamin breakdown. His question was, how many boxes of cereal did he have to eat in order to have a perfect quota of vitamins daily?

There was a long moment of silence before the expert responded that this was an extreme example of how people can misinterpret concepts! No single food will supply you with 100% of your daily vitamin and mineral requirement. Only eating a variety of real food can do that. And there's no guarantee that you can make a perfect daily selection of foods, either

Alcohol stimulates the appetite? Some people find that when they are stressed their appetite may diminish (unless they are the type that eats out of control under the same conditions!). Since alcohol can relax you, it can also turn on your appetite by reducing tension. But then, any form of relaxation would help your appetite come back; it doesn't necessarily have to be alcohol. Food also acts as a relaxant, which is one reason we eat when we're tense.

As all of us veteran dieters know, alcohol contains

calories which you just have to tack onto your intake count. Most drinks contain more than 150 calories each. It's important to understand how your body uses alcohol in order to judge whether its worth eliminating or keeping it part of your life.

As I noted, researchers have indicated that moderate intake of alcohol may help to prevent some heart disease. But that still doesn't deal with its impact on appetite.

My own experience with alcohol is that a little bit can take away my appetite. However, a little bit too much turns on my munchies and off I go. I have to be very careful. I'm not going to tell you how much is "a little bit" and how much is "a little bit too much," because it's different for everyone. Some people can put down several martinis and feel no effect. If I put that many drinks away, I'd be out like the light from a weak candle in a hurricane.

Eating just before bedtime will add pounds. The facts indicate that *when you eat has nothing to do with gaining weight.* A calorie is a calorie, by day or night. It doesn't matter when you consume it.

◆◆◆◆◆

I guess you've discovered from this section that many of the ideas people have had about getting fat and getting thin aren't true. They are just nice, comfortable excuses we use to fall back on, in order to not take responsibility for making ourselves stay overweight.

Once you give up the myths, you will be more successful n finding solutions to getting thin.

INTERMISSION
Eight Games to Play to Add Strength to your Attack

1. Buy a package of your favorite snack food. Take it to the nearest waste basket and dispose of it untouched.
2. Go to a restaurant and tell the waiter you are on a diet and to please serve you only half portions.
3. Take a long look at your favorite food that fattens and then imagine it as it will be after it's been digested.
4. Make up an absolutely outrageous tale to tell to your companion at the next meal you share in a restaurant. Such as, "I can't eat much you see, I swallowed this diamond and..."
5. Buy half-a-dozen grapefruit and make them your entire food intake for the day.
6. Fast one day a week for the hungry children of an Asian or African country and send a check for the food you would otherwise have eaten to a United Nations fund for those children.
7. Prepare a large portion of one of the foods that make you fat. Pour three tablespoons of liquid detergent over it. Now ask yourself if you want to eat it.
8. Drink four glasses of water before you take your first bite of dinner.

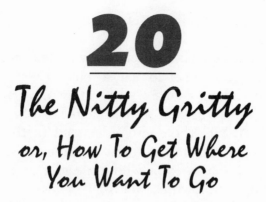

20

The Nitty Gritty
or, How To Get Where You Want To Go

We've talked about why we eat. We've talked about our cravings for certain foods. We've talked about the emotional and physical aspects of the food that goes into our bodies. We've talked about some fairly well-known diets of recent years, and how they may not be the most effective methods to reduce—*and to stay reduced.* We've also discussed being realistic about setting a goal for your weight loss.

This information is your investment in you. You are now going to lose weight by making intelligent, realistic decisions in designing your own diet. The pounds you take off now can stay off, if you use your newly acquired insight.

This time it is going to be different than all the other attempts. You promised me, and more important, you promised yourself!

This time you are going to accept responsibility before-hand for making yourself fat. That way, you can also pat yourself (and only yourself) on the back when you have made yourself thin.

Jay Kenney, Ph.D., is the nutrition specialist at the Pritikin Longevity Center in Santa Monica, California. He has a family history almost as bad as mine. By the age of thirty, Jay had a small paunch; his cholesterol was 300 and his blood pressure 140/90.

It was time for him to get serious.

He did.

Jay confessed that when he adopted good eating habits, he continued to eat a pint of Haagen Dazs Chocolate Chip ice cream every other day. He had cut down on most other fat, so he thought that he was okay.

It wasn't. His cholesterol remained in the 250-260 range. This taught him to know himself. He says: "Sure, there may be some people who can eat ice cream in small amounts once in a while. Not me.'"

Jay knew he wasn't good with temptation. He learned to keep only healthful food in his home.

"The reason I stopped eating Haagen Dazs ice cream is the same reason I don't play the lottery. It's a stupid bet."

Today his cholesterol is 160, his body fat is around ten percent and his blood pressure is down to 105/60.

Now it's time for you to know yourself. This time you are going to examine your food needs from every angle. You are going to think about what foods you feel you just "can't live without." And, you are going to try to fit these foods into your diet plan. Remember, *there are no forbidden foods, only forbidden ways to eat.*

You are going to discover when are the hungriest times of the day for you. Who invented the system where we must eat two, three or four meals a day? This is only custom and doesn't have to be adhered to as if it's a law.

While it is important to maintain a balanced approach to eating, it is not important whether you eat two, three or many meals a day.

At the Pritikin Centers, one eats six times a day—they call it grazing. You eat abundant quantities of fresh vegetables, and you're never hungry!

In some countries people eat a continental breakfast consisting of coffee or tea, a roll or pastry and maybe juice. Yet elsewhere in the world it is traditional to have a large meal to start the day.

For me, the morning is the easiest time to go without food. I'm genuinely not hungry or interested in food in the A.M. I do eat, but lightly; maybe some fruit, oatmeal and coffee or tea.

I can hear you saying, "But you have to start your day off with a good breakfast." Break out of that mold. There are no musts, as that old saying goes, except "death and taxes."

I know that most overeaters are also breakfast skippers. But there is no straight line relating those two facts. If you believe breakfast will get you off to a good start for the day, have it.

I'd rather keep mine small, and here is my reason.

I am no longer a growing girl. If I were a child whose body was still forming, I could understand the need for certain kinds of food during any single day. I also find that since I usually do my exercise in the morning, I prefer not to work out with a full stomach. Later, in mid-morning, I'll eat another small snack.

Even pediatricians now suggest that parents keep an eye on the overall food intake of children, rather than what is eaten in one particular meal, or even in one day.

For instance, if a child eats a great deal of candy or cake one day, he may compensate the next day by getting in those veggies and protein. At the end of a week, a "balanced" diet might well have been consumed.

We no longer have to be uptight about scheduling our food. Most of us eat not because we are hungry; we eat because it's lunchtime or dinnertime. If you were put in a room where there were no clocks and you couldn't tell if it was morning or evening, you would have to rely on stomach time to tell you when to eat.

Thin people eat more according to "stomach time" than to other cues like food aromas, availability and the clock. Yes, thin people are different from you and me. They eat only as much as they need to satisfy their hunger. Then they stop.

A fellow I know is one of those thin people. Before meeting him I had my own theory about thin people which was that most of them don't like desserts or similar foods that made *me* fat.

Then I met Buddy. Buddy is not only thin, but if he misses a meal he loses weight. He has to keep reminding himself to eat something or he just can't keep up his weight. (Hey, don't you hate this guy?)

I figured Buddy for one of those thin people who fit into my theory. I soon found out how wrong I was. Although some naturally thin people don't quite understand what all the fuss is about when people envy them, Buddy truly appreciates his station in life.

Buddy truly enjoys food, and especially desserts. He was particularly fond of a deep-dish strawberry pie which could be purchased only at a tiny bakery in Greenwich Village, New York. (Unfortunately for Buddy, it has gone out of business.)

When strawberry pie was available, Buddy made for the bakery and bought several. He didn't want to run short. He dug into those pies, and ate and ate. But an interesting thing happened. just as soon as Buddy was full (although because it was strawberry pie, he might eat more than usual) he put his fork down. Not because he just could not eat any more. It didn't matter whether there was pie left on his plate when he stopped.

The difference between Buddy and a fat person is that the fatty would keep eating until all the pie was gone.

Thin people eat to satisfy hunger, not appetite. They don't eat because their parents told them what good children they were if they cleared their plates. They eat because they are hungry. And, they can sometimes become so involved in activities, they forget to eat.

I'm not going to tell you that this will ever happen to you. It hasn't happened to me, and I've been thin for years.

It doesn't matter. What does matter, is realizing the difference between people who are struggling with obesity, and those who aren't.

Food has a different meaning for chronic reducers than it does for thin people whose focus is directed elsewhere. Some people, comparatively rare in number, are altogether disinterested in food. In my lifetime I have met only two, and I don't envy them.

Eating, after all, can be one of the great pleasures of life. It is for me and it will be for you, too, when you learn to control food rather than allowing food to control you.

To be totally fair, one of the two non-food people appears to like food very much. Captain J. Peter Moore was associated with Sir Alexander Korda and later, for about ten years, managed the affairs of the egocentric artist Salvador Dali.

Captain Moore happened to be an excellent cook himself. He dined in the most elegant restaurants in the western world. However, once he has a taste of the delicious food, he loses all interest. After a few bites he moves the food around on his plate so that, if you don't watch carefully, you'd believe he was eating.

The other person truly dislikes food. Remember the Jack Sprat nursery rhyme? That's her story in reverse. This woman is married to a food-obsessed fellow who is forever eating and forever trying to lose weight. When this couple married, he planned a gourmet honeymoon eating at the best restaurants unaware of his bride's antipathy to food. The scenario was lively if not pleasure-packed.

If we can focus on someone who is thin without having to diet, and observe how that person eats, we will learn that they do many of the things I suggest in this book. But they do them naturally.

For instance, they finish swallowing what is in their mouth before putting more food into it. Between bites, they put their food down (if it's something you hold in your hand like barbecued chicken). They put down the fork while they are eating, rather than impatiently waiting to shovel in more food. Watch, you'll see I'm right.

I'm going to let you in on another bit of important information. Although I consider that I have won my war against overweight, even though the war is over, the mop-up battles never end.

I must constantly remind myself of priorities. Most of the time I operate pretty much on automatic, eating sensibly. But there are also times when I need to focus myself all over again. For instance, when I wrote the paragraph about watching how thin people eat, what I was saying seemed perfectly clear. Then I had an immediate opportunity to apply that advice.

The evening I wrote the paragraph I refer to, I had a dinner engagement. By now you know how much I like desserts. So naturally, I planned to leave room for a caloric treat. Dinner was enjoyable, and I ate more than I planned of the main course. And, there just wasn't anything terrific enough in the desserts offered for me to indulge.

Fine.

Later I got home and found one cookie I'd forgotten. It was sitting in the cupboard. I decided then that it would be dessert. As I ate it, I remembered what I had written about how thin people eat. I remember how they don't stuff food into their mouths until they have finished what is already in it. They put the food down while they are chewing. And so forth.

I ate that cookie differently. I made it into an exercise on eating like a "thin" person. I took a bite, then put the cookie down and savored the flavor of what I was eating. The exercise proved to me that I could enjoy food without consuming it compulsively and unthinkingly.

What I hope I am conveying to you is that I am constantly learning and relearning about food and myself. I never will feel I know everything I need to know about staying thin, because for those of us who have been fat and want to stay thin, food can never be eaten unconsciously.

Always remember: knowledge is power. And with adequate knowledge you will have the power to reduce and remain thin. And you can do this all the rest of your life.

I guarantee it.

Realistic Goals

When I was at my fattest, I swung back and forth like a pendulum about my weight goals. First, I wanted to be 100 pounds. It seemed like a nice easy number to remember. At other times I felt it would be impossible for me to lose more than ten, maybe fifteen pounds.

When you are heavy it seems impossible to become what you believe is really thin. It's also difficult to accept anything less than a weight that is probably impossible to achieve.

Of course, by setting your goals this high it makes it impossible to do anything, so you eat another sandwich and think about it.

How do we set a realistic goal? First, I'll tell you how not to set one. My girlfriend used to watch the Miss America beauty pageant each year. When they announced the measurements of each contestant, my friend enjoyed comparing her weight to that of the young ladies competing to become the number one popular symbol of physical perfection.

If that year produced a large number of ladies whose weight was close to my friend's weight she would rationalize herself out of trying to take off those pounds she normally believed did not belong on her body. "If Miss America and I are the same weight, I must be okay."

(Naturally, she did not bother to comment on whether or not the weight looked different when it was distributed on Miss America. Or whether the potential Miss America was five inches taller than she was.)

We often set goals according to the measurements of people we admire. I can recall poring over magazine articles about some of my favorite movie stars which occasionally mentioned their weight. If it was a low figure I decided that if it was good enough for Miss Movie Star, it would be perfect for me.

I didn't consider how the movie star's weight would have looked on my frame.

Apart from that obvious juvenile manner of deciding on a goal, here is another reason why patterning your weight after someone else's is unrealistic.

I grew up admiring Elizabeth Taylor. I still believe she is one of the world's most beautiful women. When she was young she could take your breath away. As she matured her beauty remained, but her body got out of hand. One magazine article mentioned her weight. It was a surprisingly low figure.

My God! If Elizabeth Taylor weighed that and looked considerably overweight what on earth did I look like, weighing ten pounds more!

When I read that article it never occurred to me that maybe the figure was not quite accurate. Maybe it was an affectionately written piece and thus understated her weight. I believed every word, especially about her weight.

Overweight people spend the greater part of a week getting on and off of the scale. Digital scales can tell us to the tenth of a pound how much we weigh. Were they trying to tell me that Elizabeth Taylor did not weigh as little as that article suggested?

Well, who really cares how much Elizabeth Taylor weighs? Except Elizabeth Taylor. Soon enough Elizabeth Taylor reached a point in her life when she decided to do something about her extra pounds. Unfortunately, no matter how much she reduces, she hasn't managed to stay thin. But we can identify with her struggle.

How are you going to figure out how much you ought to weigh? The first step is to look at yourself as you are now. Get in front of a mirror, naked. That's right, strip down to skin. Don't look away. This may be the first time you've taken a good look at yourself in a long time. Examine every inch. This is a critical look, so don't expect that you are going to be thrilled with what you see.

Hold in your stomach. Nothing happens, right? Still there. Turn around and look at your rear too. Use a hand mirror and slowly scrutinize your body .

How long have you been in the shape you see? A few months? Years? Have you been carrying that excess weight ever since childhood? Did you put on weight during pregnancy and never take it off? Was your pregnancy fifteen years ago? Did you gain weight after you stopped smoking? When did you stop smoking? (My ex-husband used that excuse for two years!)

Now get dressed. The examination is over—temporarily. A grown person should have to endure just so much punishment.

Boy, are you lucky!

Yes, lucky, because you now have a clear-cut job to do that will bring you a great sense of accomplishment.

When you set your goal, think about the questions I asked. How long have you been fat? That's important. Because you must realize that you are not going to get thin overnight. *If you have been carrying around excess pounds for a long time you must set a reasonable goal that will insure success.*

In setting your goal, be realistic about something else. Certain aspects about you can never be changed, no matter how much weight you lose. Your body type and shape are with you forever.

In 1940, Dr. W. H. Sheldon categorized all bodies into three types. The ectomorph is the guy who is long and lanky. The mesomorph is more rectangular or pear shaped, with sturdy arms and legs. The curvy endomorph is more rounded, tending towards the plump. That was more than half a century ago, and we still accept these universal categories

We all fit into one or another of them with some overlapping. However, as long as you believe that losing weight is going to reshape your basic structure, you are headed for nothing but frustration.

To give you a different analogy, it would never occur to you to try to become two inches taller than you are. You accept your height because you know you can't change it, even if you'd prefer being taller or shorter. However, with your figure it's somewhat different. it is true that when you reduce you eventually reduce everywhere. But I came to peace with myself long ago over the fact that no matter how thin I get, I'll always have thighs that are a little bit bigger proportionately than the rest of me. This is a fact of life it's best to learn to live with. It'll help you be happier about accepting yourself when you get to your goal.

If your goal is to lose one hundred pounds in two months you are not going to be able to do it . No way. But if you tell yourself that in one month you want to be five pounds lighter, your chances are very good that you will succeed.

If you think five pounds is not satisfactory for one month, you are getting impatient. And impatience is nonproductive. If you have a lot of weight to lose, develop the attitude that you are going to reduce in stages.

No one can lose one hundred pounds all at once. But if you figure out how much weight you will lose in one year if you reduce five pounds each month, you'll discover that adds up to sixty pounds. (Okay, it's not one hundred pounds, but sixty punds is a lot of weight to lose in one year.)

If you set your goal in that fashion you can succeed. How about a loss of as little as one pound a week? Nothing? It's a reasonable, manageable goal to accomplish. Losing four pounds a month is a snap. It's so easy you'll wonder why you struggled and agonized all these years. One pound a week? Of course you can do it!]

Not fast enough, my fat friend? You want to raise your goal to eight or twelve pounds a month? Take heed. Have you been able to maintain any of the weight lost on crash programs? And if you had begun to lose a pound a week one year ago, today you would be *fifty-two pounds lighter.*

An acquaintance of mine who had been skinny most of her life suddenly was thirty pounds overweight. She found out she had hypoglycemia. This condition caused intense sugar cravings, which she'd indulged.

Never having had to diet before, my friend went to her physician. He put her on a program which had her reducing very slowly. As a matter of fact, if she lost more than the one and one-half pounds a week, as prescribed, he adjusted her menu by adding food.

While you are setting this "easy" goal, remember, too, that there will be weeks when you will not lose weight. You are human, not a machine. You can't actually "walk off" a piece of apple pie by figuring out how many calories you "burn" by walking. Your body is too complicated a mechanism. But if your goal is one pound a week and you stumble one week, you'll catch up in the next stretch. It's reachable and healthy. Don't allow one brief failure to discourage you into giving up and bingeing.

Now, in case you haven't gotten my message, like most things in life it's quite simple. When you go on a "diet" you start and, at some point, you finish. It has a beginning and an end. And when the fat lady has sung and it's over, it's over.

What I'm proposing is in stark contrast to a formal diet. I'm directing you to change your attitudes as well as your eating habits.

There is no end to this. And, as the weight comes off gradually, you are altering yourself and your food attitudes. As weeks and months pass, you realize that since there is no end to this approach, you are embracing a permanent way of life. The weight loss is gradual. The lifestyle change is gradual. There is danger that when you come to the flag which reads "Finish Line" you will revert to your old eating habits. Remember, those have become your old eating habits!

◆◆◆◆◆

Very important for women:

What with premenstrual, menstrual and post menstrual periods, women sometimes find themselves having more difficulty losing weight at different times of the month. Moreover, women can be extremely discouraged to discover a temporary weight *gain* from water retention at these times, even though they know they haven't been overeating.

It's important to plan for these times when you seem not to be losing. If you know they are going to occur, you won't look at them as setbacks because they will be part of your total strategy.

For instance, if I were setting my goal and it was four pounds a month, I'd go one step further. I would remind myself, perhaps by writing it on a calendar, that when my period was due I would not lose weight, and might even gain.

The menstrual cycle is not a constant either. There's no guarantee that each month you will retain fluids around that time. Sometimes it happens and sometimes it doesn't. However, if you plan not to lose during that time, you can only feel delighted if you drop weight.

It's all part of the little game we learn to play with ourselves. You must never ever kid yourself, but you can learn to pretend or just not pay attention and then be pleased with a positive result.

To go even further, during the time just prior to and during my menstruation, I would determine not to get on the scale. This is difficult. There is a fine line separating positive and negative motivation, and only you know when you've stepped across it.

There are times when I know my weight is up and then I decide to weigh myself. When I make the decision it's because I know that seeing the number will startle me into getting the weight off. However, there are other times when I know my weight is up and I will not go near the scale. I know that those are times when weighing myself will not be productive, and might make me depressed enough to binge. So, I avoid the scale.

Get to know your body and your psyche. Discover the days when you seem to have more difficulty reducing. Get an overview by comparing one month to another. See if you can't establish a pattern that will give you insight. If you accomplish this you will not only lose weight, you will feel very much in control of yourself. You won't think some outside forces are working against you, making it difficult to lose.

Even if you don't have fifty-two pounds to lose, set your goal with the future in mind. If you want to lose twenty pounds use the same principles. Don't expect to lose all the weight at once. Don't even try. Don't crash diet. *The pounds you lose on a crash diet will not stay off!*

Break that pattern of three days eating and three days dieting. This time, keep in mind your promise to be realistic, whether it's one hundred pounds, twenty pounds or five pounds. This time you are not going to lose fast and repent slowly.

Yes, plateaus will occur when you won't seem to lose any weight. A plateau is a time when your body is readjusting to your new weight. There are times when your weight won't budge. You can actually learn to enjoy the plateau and make that period a positive one. After all, you are thinner than you were, so you can congratulate yourself for accomplishing that.

Learn to use plateaus to your advantage.

Marking your calendar and plotting your weight loss can keep you in touch with your overall success. The finish line is always surprisingly near.

As you approach your goal, prepare yourself to enjoy and accept your new figure. Learn to accept the compliments you are going to receive. Resist the temptation to tell everyone how fat you used to be.

Teach yourself to be delighted with the new you. Be content with your chosen goal if it is still reasonable. Be aware of the danger at this point of trying to reduce more than you believe you really need to. Don't become a compulsive dieter.

Now you know how to select your goal. Whether it's 150, 200, 40 or 10 pounds. You've taken out your calendar and marked down how much weight you expect to lose as well as the realistic rate at which you expect to reduce. Remember, you're not going to get any thinner than the goal you set for yourself.

There's yet another important step.

Make time for more introspection. Yes, you still have to learn more about yourself so that you can decide just which approach will be especially helpful in your individual weight loss program.

Get to know yourself and forget why your neighbor seems to be losing when she also seems to be eating pizza all the time, while you subsist on starvation rations.

She isn't you. And you aren't her.

Leave your ego in the closet and accept the opinions and comments of your friends as well intentioned. Pick someone you love and trust, whom you know feels the same about you. Thus, you won't interpret your friend's observations as criticism.

Pay particular attention to what triggers eating. Do you find yourself getting up from your chair at every television commercial and hitting the nibbles? When I come home from work, immediately after I hang up my coat I head for the kitchen.

It's quite normal for people to be hungry in the late afternoon or early evening. After all, it's been several hours since lunch and it's not quite dinnertime. It's actually danger time.

If you know this is your pattern make up your mind to change it by *not* going to the kitchen. Instead, go directly to the bathroom. Don't even put your coat away. Brush your teeth. This activity will act to clean your palate and give you the time you need to make a conscious decision about whether or not you want to go into the kitchen.

If you don't do this, and find yourself in the kitchen, prepare foods that are on hand for immediate grabbing. These should be foods and beverages that won't add weight.

You might find that the refrigerator is not your enemy. Instead, the villain may be the pantry where you stash the crackers or potato chips.

Unlike Jay Kenney, I do keep goodies in my home. I've learned I can handle them. But I deliberately move these to the top shelf so that to reach them I must climb a stepladder. The moment's interval between climbing and reaching often makes all the difference for me to become acutely aware that this is not what I want to be doing.

I keep certain foods in the refrigerator which are the first thing I see when I open the door. These are carrot sticks, celery, radishes, etc. They may not nourish my spirit, but they do my figure just dandy.

For years you have eaten the way you do, and it makes you fat. If you don't change that, you will get fat again.

People who lose weight on a liquid protein diet are learning nothing about their relationship to food and the world. Unless they learn, zoom! on go the pounds. Eating bananas and milk for a month will make you lose weight. So will Grape Nuts cereal and an apple, three times a day.

Even a one-sided diet like ice cream only will result in weight loss. But are you prepared to spend the rest your life sipping liquid protein, or eating bananas and milk? Any weight reduction program must include foods you feel you can eat over an extended period of time.

You can plan your own program which will be quite different from the next person's. Don't forget, no food is forbidden. It's the way you handle it that you have to watch.

I eat better now than I ever did when I was fat. When I was fat I was nondiscriminating about food. I am very selective now because I know I'll get fat again if I return to my old habits. Once you have developed better food habits and learn to enjoy food it's difficult to be satisfied with junk.

Snobbish?

Maybe.

But it works for me.

Let's determine what will work for you.

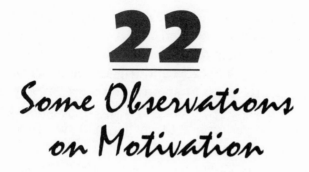

22

Some Observations on Motivation

Some insurance companies are becoming aware that they can motivate people to lose weight.

Some years ago the Admire Group, a Santa Ana, California, insurance company, proposed a contract where employees agreed to participate for a year in trying to lose at least fifteen pounds.

Employees had the option of taking behavior modification classes at a local hospital. If they lost the minimum number of pounds (there was no maximum limit), the fee for the course was reimbursed by the company. And for each pound of weight they lost, the company paid them $3!

Until someone offers you a similar deal, you'll have to supply your own motivation. Maybe just looking and feeling like a million is reward enough.

There are people who think they are accomplishing something positive by taking diuretics to help them reduce. Diuretics help excrete excess water our bodies may hold from time to time. These are frequently used by women during that bloaty time of their menstrual cycle.

If you depend upon water loss to get thin, you are only kidding yourself. And you will be discouraged after you "gain" it all back in the course of simply drinking water. Getting rid of water is not losing fat.

There is the additional real risk of losing potassium, so diuretics shouldn't be taken casually. You can put yourself in danger. For instance, diuretics can raise your uric acid count to dangerous levels and trigger the onset of gout.

This brings to mind an amusing story about water. A fun-loving publisher I know could only get motivated to diet if it involved competition. He had two friends who were massively overweight too so it was easy to get a wager going. The plan was to weigh in, nude, each week and whoever lost the most would be paid $10 a pound by the other two.

The sly fellow figured all was fair in love, war and weight reduction contests. He knew how to win. The evening before the first weigh-in, he started drinking water. He drank glass after glass.

He continued in the morning until his friends arrived. He literally could hear the water sloshing around in his stomach. He had to urinate in the worst way, but he was determined not to until they had all weighed in.

When the others arrived they stripped down. They didn't notice my friend's discomfort. He even offered them a can of diet soda which they refused. Then, each of the three got on the scale.

The other two were skeptical. They couldn't believe that my friend weighed as much as the scale read. "You don't have metal weights between your toes?" they asked. But since they were all nude, they could detect nothing fishy.

After they left, my friend quickly made for the bathroom to relieve himself. The next weigh-in was scheduled for the following Friday. As my friend saw it, he could eat as much as he liked and still "win" the bet since he had managed to drink fourteen pounds' worth of water.

The following Friday my friend did, indeed, "win" his bet. But he was just kidding himself.

It's an amusing story, but I hope the point is clear. My friend didn't take off any weight.

Don't kid yourself. If you aren't honest, all your effort will be wasted. Had my friend used his energy for dieting he might have lost the bet but won, by losing pounds. If you want to continue fooling yourself, put this book away and postpone your plans to get thin until you can accept the truth.

Better to accept yourself as fat than to keep trying and not succeeding, blaming forces other than yourself. A variation of the above trick is frequently used by pregnant women. I recall my first visit to the obstetrician after learning of my pregnancy. Part of the routine during visits was a monthly weigh-in.

Although there has been some difference of opinion about how much weight a woman should gain while she is pregnant, at the time I was carrying my child, getting very heavy was discouraged. An eighteen to twenty pound weight gain was considered ideal.

On that first visit there was another woman in the waiting room with me. Her dress consisted of many different layers of clothing. She seemed to be perspiring due to the weight of her garments.

I asked her if she wasn't uncomfortable dressed that way. "Sure," she replied, "but I want to weigh in heavy this month so that next month, even if I gain weight, I'll still be ahead."

Ahead of what?

I discovered other women who would crash diet the week before their weigh-in with the doctor for the same purpose.

Not only do they deceive themselves, they may be cheating their unborn child. During pregnancy, it's particularly important for women to maintain a balanced diet. That's one time you don't want to be on a reducing plan, unless your physician feels that you are overweight to start out. And then, you must work with him.

If you want to play tricks, use the ones that will *help*

you lose weight and not be merely the illusion of accomplishment. By now you have learned many hints that can help you reduce.

In the next chapter we will concentrate on even more "tricks" that can work for you—and make losing weight a winning experience. They can make the difference between staying where you are, and getting thinner.

INTERMISSION

Winning the Restaurant Game

1. Never eat in a restaurant that offers an "all you can eat" buffet
2. If there is bread and butter on the table, ask the waiter to remove them
3. Order á la carte (Don't order a "complete lunch" or "complete dinner.")
4. Once in a while, order two appetizers and skip the main course.
5. Be the last person at your table to start eating.
6. Eat something, perhaps a light snack, before a party, a dinner out, etc., to keep you from uncontrolled eating.

23

Tricks of the Trade-Off

So you really want to get thin? You want to learn all those little things that make it easier? I remind you again that I didn't promise it would be easy, did I? It's never really easy.

But it is possible. It takes preparation, and often it takes a sense of humor.

If you remember that you are always trading one thing off for another more desirable thing you'll get the idea. Trading off some foods and undisciplined eating habits for more positive behavior and a better figure makes the trade worth it.

I will recite a bag full of tricks; some of them I believe will work and others I don't have much faith in. However, I'll give you my opinion as well as that of other people who do think they help. You'll be able to pick and choose from the lot.

Remember walking? How about walking up a flight of stairs instead of taking the elevator even if you can only make it one floor. Walk down if walking up doesn't appeal to you. It may not be much, but it's something.

If you drop something, retrieve it effectively. By that I mean either with deep knee bends, turning an accident into an exercise. (Entertainer Rita Moreno uses this as a regular part of her fitness program.)

Once in a while walk to one destination where you

would normally take your car. It saves gas and gets you moving.

Or, at a shopping mall, park as far from the entrance as possible. Use the walk to and from your car as exercise.

It's been observed that even a little bit of exercise is better than none. Robert Pritikin, who took over the leadership of the Pritikin Longevity Center from his father, often refers to "Pritikin Light"—those days when you don't have time to do a full workout. Doing something is better than doing nothing.

Keep a picture of yourself in your wallet. A real fat one. If you can't bear the thought of someone discovering it, cut off the head. No one will ever guess it's you. Look at it from time to time, especially when some tempting food is in sight.

Forget about pasting a photo of yourself on the refrigerator door or little signs that say things like DON'T BE A DIET DROPOUT. They soon became invisible. If you do want to hang up a picture, choose one where you look great. (This will obviously work only if you have such a photo available!)

Try to eat all your meals in one specific place. This is more difficult than it sounds but if you combine it with the excellent advice to never eat standing up, it's even tougher—and better!

Not eating while standing up immediately eliminates ice cream cones while strolling, pizza from a fast-food counter, hot-dog stand—a giant leap forward.

Apply the rule at home too. The next time you find yourself nibbling on a potato chip, or even a carrot stick, make sure you sit down at the dining room table.

The point of this is to make eating conscious behavior. If you force yourself to eat only at the table, you must also become aware of the unconscious eating you do. Consciously or unconsciously, it all counts.

Do you know any of the many mothers who turn

themselves into human garbage pails? Those are the ones who finish their kids' meals. Half a peanut butter and jelly sandwich here, four French fries there. Then they can't understand how they became fat because they "never eat lunch." They never eat their own lunch, that is.

Concentrate on your eating. Eat slowly. *Taste* the food. Don't read while eating. *Never* eat while watching television.

One trick I used for years is something I used to be somewhat embarrassed about. Until I met other people who do it, too. Moreover, it's recommended by behavior modification experts! Use small plates and utensils. I'll put my food on a little plate and use a small cake fork instead of a large one. That way my smaller portion of food doesn't look lost.

If you can manipulate them, use chopsticks. Not only will it slow you down at first, but you'll become accustomed to eating smaller amount of food rather than stuffing your mouth.

Try switching eating hands. If you are right handed, eat with the left, and vice versa.

How about serving yourself exactly one half of the normal portion you usually eat? Then, if you want second helpings, your second portion will actually be the last half of your first portion.

If some of these suggestions sound funny, save your laughter until you've tried them. You'll find they work. While you're laughing, remember to put down your fork between bites, and swallow before putting more food into your mouth.

I'm sounding more and more like your mother, aren't I?

Except you must retrain the bad eating habits that you learned as a child. It's amazing how unaware of them you are until you start trying to change.

More advice: prepare your plate in the kitchen and put on it the quantity of food you want to eat. some people suggest that you cook only that amount. This is not always realistic. It's kind of hard to roast six ounces of beef at a time. But it is possible to put that amount on your plate, carry it into the dining room and sit down at the table to eat it.

Wrap and store all leftovers immediately after you have served yourself. Don't make it easy to help yourself to seconds.

Don't put platters of food on the table. If you decide you want more, you'll have to get up and go into the kitchen to get it. You may still choose to have that second portion, but you will have made a conscious decision to do so.

Here's another one. Do not eat unless you are hungry. In the early part of this book I told you how efficient my body is just before I find I'm hungry. The world-famous Hindu leader, Mahatma Gandhi, said: "An empty stomach is one of the secrets of any creativity."

You may not find your creative juices flowing because of an empty belly, but your gastric juices will start up. It's probably a long time since you've even allowed it to go to half empty. Most of us eat not because we're hungry, but because it's "time to eat." This is one habit we can break.

One of the pleasures of being an adult is that no one tells you when to eat. You're the boss. If you don't feel like eating, don't. You will find yourself hungrier for your meals, and you will enjoy them more even while you eat less because the food is truly functioning as fuel.

It could be difficult for people who travel frequently from country to country to follow the advice just offered. remember that there are great time differences. A friend of mine solved that problem by eating only according to his local time. This sometimes means he gets hungry at three in the morning. But he finds that if he does not do this he constantly throws his body off.

Your problem is not that of a jet traveler. You just want

to start recognizing the symptoms of being hungry.

I described how I find myself going right to the kitchen when I arrive home from work. Although I try to keep things available that are good for me to eat, it's even better when I distract myself with some other activity.

How often have you eaten something so quickly you didn't have a chance to think about it? It went down so fast you hardly tasted it. When you learn that it takes the body twenty minutes to "register" the food you've consumed, you can see how impulsive eating is something we very much want to avoid.

Before you've reminded yourself that you shouldn't, you already have consumed a handful of peanuts, a chocolate brownie, etc. If you can get yourself out of the rooms containing food and give yourself enough time to plan, you'll be on the way to cutting down on these impulses.

How about skipping a meal? Television personality Bill Boggs finds dinner easiest to eliminate. Go to bed early once a week and poof, no dinner. You'll be pleased the next morning when your tight jeans are a little looser.

You might even skip eating entirely one day a week. Do I hear a gasp? Many of our most fashionable people believe in this as a way to revive the body after an especially full weekend. You may recall I used to fast on Mondays after stuffing myself all weekend long. You don't have to be overfed in order to do this. Drink lots of water during the fast day.

I read about one woman who expands on this by spending the entire day in bed. She feels like a little girl playing hooky from her responsibilities, but she loves it. Her magazines and books and telephone are on the bed, and on a table nearby is a large bottle of mineral water. All day long she sips from the bottle.

Of course, this is not practical for those of us who have a houseful of children, dogs, cats and spouses. But we can try to save one portion of each day just for ourselves.

Skipping dinner (or lunch, or breakfast for that matter) or fasting for one day doesn't sound like a punishment when you have it described as above. It should be a mini-respite, one that you will enjoy trying.

Select a time during the day or evening when you usually get the munchies. Make a pact with yourself that today you will not succumb. You needn't commit yourself beyond one day. That's punishment enough. This is intended to be a positive experience. You will learn that you can do it and you'll feel good when you have done it. Just once. It's a contract you are making with yourself. If you want to re-negotiate tomorrow, fine. If not, try something else.

In a pamphlet entitled *The Psychology of Dieting,* H. Jon Geis, Ph.D., points out that "can't" nearly always means "won't" or "haven't."

In other words, you are more able to be successful and even to withstand the stress involved in reducing if you discard the concept "I can't."

Dr. Geis says, "It is useful to think in terms of 'I won't' instead of 'I can't' as a way of showing yourself that you do have the power to diet successfully if you want to. The word 'can't' implies a 100 percent prediction with certainty."

If you keep telling yourself "I can't," you probably will be unsuccessful. You are establishing a conclusion before you even start. If you tell yourself "I haven't" that at least leaves open the possibility that you will succeed.

Do you realize that by trying your own combination of these hints once, you'll make progress in losing weight and probably never be bored? I believe strongly in varying your routine so you are constantly stimulated in a forward direction. Boredom is a major contributor to overeating.

Varying your routine will avoid that trap.

More games: Make it difficult for yourself to overeat. If you live alone, keep very little food in the house. If you want food, go out and buy it. One day, take only enough money with you to buy a piece of fruit for lunch.

Focus your mind on *trying* to succeed. If your focus is on *trying* rather than on *succeeding* you reduce the tension and anxiety that can develop when too much importance is placed on success. Don't worry about succeeding. If you follow my advice, winning will take care of itself.

Further, if your aim is only to try, you won't be devastated when you occasionally don't live up to your promise.

What's that? Failure? Look, we're human beings. We got fat because we sometimes lose control. You may fall off the wagon occasionally. Later, I'll tell you how to get off a binge. For the moment, I want you to accept yourself, warts and all.

Accepting yourself means also accepting the fact that sometimes it will seem like your plan is falling apart. It's not, really. There are moments when you can try to find out what's really bothering you instead of ignoring your problems by eating.

Overeating will be part of us for a long time; maybe forever. Lots of people still occasionally overeat but manage to stay thin. Because you have been accustomed to being heavy, you might believe that any time you lose control it means total failure. This is not so. Just as you did not make yourself fat with one isolated moment of overeating, remember too that losing control once in a while is not going to put all the weight back on you.

I can't tell you how many dieters want to throw in the towel because they've had a dessert at dinner. One reason for this reaction is dieters think they are being "good" if they don't have any of the foods they believe make them fat.

By now you know that no food makes you fat. You make you fat. Think of the quantity of food you would need to *keep* you fat, and you'll get the idea.

The feeling of deprivation is one which short-circuits many dieters. If you believe that dieting means you are never going to be able to eat your favorite foods you certainly will feel deprived. However, if you *plan* to include them in your diet, you won't feel deprived. If you want that dessert, *plan* to eat it occasionally. Look forward to it. You'll undoubtedly enjoy it more than you ever did when you ate it unconsciously. And it won't make you fat. Having fulfilled your desire, you can continue losing.

You may be surprised to discover that once the bugaboo of fear is off "treat" foods, you may not desire to eat them in the quantities you previously did when you were in your uncontrolled state. Now that you don't have to "steal " that treat, a little may go a long way.

Don't forget, when you decide to eat a favorite food, *trade it off against something else.* You can't have it all, but if you enjoy one food more than another, it's worth making the exchange. Most thin people eat this way. For them it's automatic.

Deprivation is a negative force; reducing is a positive one. *When you have reduced you will feel good about yourself.* Every step you take to lose pounds should make you feel that you are taking a positive action. The feeling will sustain your effort and will propel you forward.

Control can be a positive force in your life. Look upon controlled eating as beneficial. If you don't agree with me, think about the uncontrolled eating you have done and recall how unhappy you were about it - the unhappiness is not only after the binge.

If you think about spending the rest of your life on a diet, the thought will depress you. But if you think of gaining control of your eating and, thus, your life, you can look forward to great and good feelings with possible serendipitous rewards.

Compulsive eating and belly-filling bingeing are

uncontrolled. I've never met anyone who claims to really enjoy the experience. The morning after—even the hour after—is often miserable. You are filled with self-recrimination and an abiding sense of failure.

Let's continue to examine the positives.

Do you weigh yourself too often? There are many theories about weighing. I have tested all of them from weighing myself every day to weighing myself every time I go to the bathroom, to weighing myself once a week.

At this point in my life, I hardly ever weigh myself. Why not? I don't need the scale to tell me what I already know.

Want to know something? It doesn't matter. When we thin out, the evidence will be there, whether or not we see a number recorded in front of our eyes. People go nutty about scales and their messages.

When I subscribed to the daily weigh-in regime, I would get on the scale at the same time each day, completely stripped, after going to the bathroom.

Weight is relative and scales vary. Don't panic when you step on someone else's scale and see a different number than you saw on your own.

Think of your scale as an old friend. Consider it "correct" because you weigh yourself only on your own scale. The fact is, it doesn't matter if the scale is "right" or "wrong" since it is the only one you'll use.

Discover what's best for you and keep in mind that your weight will fluctuate, not only weekly and daily, but within the day, too. (After eating, I can "weigh" four pounds more!)

Whether or not you weigh yourself, if you are eating according to your food plan, you are winning. The number on the scale is not the point. Getting thin is.

24

You're Going to be Eating

You are going to be eating, so let's discuss—rather than avoid—food. Start with your own special favorites. Some people enjoy cottage cheese and grapefruit while others cringe at the sight of either one of them.

I can eat pasta every day. If you can too, prepare a different (or the same, if you wish) pasta meal for every day of the week. It may bore someone else, but for you it's perfect. Next week, switch to a different food. For me, chicken is another favorite, as well as purely vegetarian meals. If I don't include your favorites, substitute them.

If you are lucky enough and rich enough you can prepare a simple 500-calorie meal with a baked potato topped off by a generous dollop of Beluga caviar.

If you can afford shrimp, lobster, caviar, steak (lean cuts, please) you'll see what I mean. Of course, fish (not so cheap anymore, either), chicken, tuna fish, cottage cheese, and eggs are also available. But please watch your cholesterol level, if it's a concern for you.

When I separated from my first husband and decided to drop some weight, I ate just about the same thing every day. It was either a steak and salad or a large hamburger and salad, depending on my budget. (That was in my pre-Pritikin life!)

The effectiveness of this menu was largely due to its

monotony. Although I've warned you that boredom and deprivation can lead to going off your diet, in this case, it was my choice, not a program forced on me. *Choice* is the important difference.

This will only work for those of you for whom varying your menu leads to an over-concentration about food. If you are going to think all day about how you might create a masterpiece out of 350 calories, I hope you can change your focus away from food to other interests.

Think about whether eating the same, albeit nutritious, menu for one week straight will bore the life out of you, and make you crave hot fudge sundaes. If your answer is yes, go for variety. However, if eating the same food eliminates thinking about and worrying over what you'll have for dinner, this may be an effective approach.

Don't make it absurd—don't eat only strawberries and pickled herring. Make sure you select foods that will nourish your body. You can pick foods you genuinely like. Today I'd substitute a huge baked potato and salad for the steak or hamburger. Make your own choices makes for enjoyment; when someone else decides for you it can lead to feeling deprived. *Your involvement is what makes the critical difference.*

By planning in advance that you will eat an eight-ounce hamburger and a green salad with oil and vinegar, you won't hurt yourself one bit. And, if you like, toss in a glass of red wine. Light a candle, put on the stereo and have a pleasant time.

As you might be able to tell, I very enthusiastically endorse this approach. If you want variety, do it on a change-the-menu-each-week basis.

Keep foremost in mind that your goal is to lose weight, not to plan menus.

When I was a youngster attending junior high school, I ate cream cheese and jelly sandwiches every school day for one solid year. I guess I was cut out for this lifestyle. I can still taste those sandwiches and enjoy their memory. (By the way, I haven't had a cream cheese and jelly sandwich since then!)

If you care to, figure out a menu that contains the precise number of calories you want to consume daily.

Write it down.

Make it a simple one.

Eat the same menu for one week.

Many dieters respond well to the above since it takes the day-to-day or meal-to-meal planning out of their hands.

Taking the surprise element out of food is helpful when you want to lose weight. Part of this approach is to make food seem less important in the full scope of your life. In time, when you have won the battle against your bulges, you can be more flexible. But at the beginning it's safer to know in advance what's going down.

It may turn you into a person who starts looking at the rest of the world instead of only restaurants, food articles, and the like. You will find yourself not thinking just about dinner, and maybe planning instead what film to see, or what book you are going to read.

Dining is an incredibly social activity. Thus, when behavior modification specialists tell us to make eating an isolated experience, they're asking a great deal.

Just as I don't think it is a solution to go to a spa and lose weight under controlled conditions, I also concede that making eating a "pure" experience may not work for you. So, if you *must* watch TV or read a newspaper while eating—make sure your quantity controls are firmly set first.

This reminds me of a friend whose excuse for not dieting is that he has to go to a spa and isolate himself, if he is to diet. But what happens when he comes out of isolation?

The sooner you learn to lose weight right in the middle of the real world, the sooner you're going to win the war. Needing to be isolated is only another cop out. When I was a Weight Watcher—at my fattest—I managed to lose weight, even though, as I mentioned, it was in the middle of the Thanksgiving and Christmas holiday season.

If you are motivated, it doesn't matter where you are. You can be sitting in a pool of Swiss butter almond ice cream surrounded by mounds of Almond Joy candy bars, platters of hot pizza and mountains of Black Forest chocolate cake, and they will all seem like chunks of dead wood to you.

I concede that it's practically unpatriotic to not socialize with people unless there is food available. Think about the last time you were invited out to a friend's home. Did you sit and enjoy each other's company without nibbling? At what hour were coffee and cake served? Or was the event a party where the onset of the food platters seemed to be the high-point of the evening?

It would probably start a small revolution to suggest to people that they can relate without watching each other chew. Care to join me in a peaceful revolution?

Relax. You don't have to struggle to change the world. All you need change is yourself. You are going to learn how to live with food and still lose weight.

If you find you need support on a one-to-one basis I highly recommend consulting a behavior modification specialist. It's becoming more popular for physicians to work together with such experts since these are the people who are trained in nutrition and who can help tailor a reducing regime to your particular needs.

Where most diets fail is that they don't take you further than the weight loss. However, if your weight reduction program is designed with foods that you can continue eating after the weight is off, you're headed for the Winner's Circle.

Behavior modification is important enough to merit a separate chapter. However before we talk more about modifying your behavior, let's do more plain talking about food.

I'm deliberately not advocating that you eat specific foods or recommending one reducing approach over another because I want you to be able to make decisions for yourself.

I keep stressing that no one food or diet program will work for everyone. Your needs and desires are probably different from mine, so it's not fair for me to tell you that every day you will eat certain foods and then you'll be thin.

Instead, I have encouraged you to select those foods you enjoy eating. If you include them in your reducing program, you will lose weight without sacrificing pleasurable eating.

Most important of all, the foods you choose will be foods that you'll be able to continue to eat after you lose weight.

25
More Talk About Food

Occasionally I'll read through a supposed "diet" food recipe for cheesecake or the like. There are so many substitutes for ingredients that would make you fat, you end up with an imitation more at home in a chemistry laboratory than a kitchen.

My philosophy, as you know by now, is that there are no forbidden foods. Only forbidden ways to eat them. With that in mind, I suggest you have cheesecake if you want it. Good cheesecake is too delicious to mess around with substitutes. If you think you ought not eat it now, wait until you feel you can.

Good things are worth waiting for. The fake is just that: fake.

And while you're at it, don't fool yourself about "natural" foods. People are too impressed when they see a package labeled "natural," believing it must be good for them. Dr. Scrimshaw, whom I quoted earlier, says the notion that such foods are safe is "a total myth."

He adds, "A surprisingly high percentage of the food we eat and think of as natural has toxic substances that wouldn't pass the rat tests required of all additives. A list of these substances includes hemagglutinins in beans, cyanogenic glycosides in almonds and lima beans, pressor amines in bananas, pineapples, lemons, tomatoes, sauer-

kraut juice, Stilton and Camembert cheeses and even natural radioactivity in some drinking water."

Whatever these things are, I don't want them in my
body!

I'm not asking you to toss in the towel completely on
"natural" foods, but don't be fooled into thinking they are
going to save you or the rest of the world.

There are now many "natural" and "health food"
stores. Have you ever wondered how natural some of
them are? Not far from my home there is one such shop.
You can find natural vitamins, natural cookies, sprouts
and so forth. Even natural and organically grown fresh
vegetables. And not surprisingly, these foods frequently
cost a lot more than "unnatural" ones.

A neighbor shopped in this store often. She developed
a personal friendship with the woman who owned the
shop. One morning when my neighbor was browsing in
the shop, the owner took my friend aside. Evidencing
some discomfort, she advised my neighbor not to buy carrots. When asked why, the natural health food store
owner revealed that they were purchased at the local
supermarket—not from an organic farm.

I suppose she felt guilty that day and decided to save
my friend the considerable difference it would have cost
since the carrots were marked up to the suitable "natural"
price.

I do not mean to suggest that all, or even many of
these shops are run this way. However, you might be surprised at how many perfectly acceptable products you can
find right in your supermarket.

Some dieters decide that becoming vegetarian is going
to solve all their weight problems, and, at the same time,
they'll be "healthier." While it is certainly true that you
can get all the nutrition you need through a vegetarian
diet (proteins can be derived from many foods other than
animal flesh—milk, cheese, whole grains, etc.) don't

think that you will become thin automatically. There are plenty of overweight vegetarians. Some of them eat their way through huge masses of nuts, refined grains, etc., and these will put on pounds.

Vegetarianism is fine, if it's comfortable for you. I find myself eating less beef and other red meats, partly because they contain more calories and partly because they are frequently the most expensive items you can buy. However, I'm not committed to any "ism" when it comes to food.

Keep in mind the critical point I've tried to make again and again. For your food program to be effective, it must be one that you'll be satisfied living with for years to come. If you think vegetarianism fits that bill try it.

Vegetarian cooks frequently are very creative since they need to invent interesting ways to prepare the foods they buy. I believe one reason many of us are "meat and potatoes people" is because it's somehow simpler to grill a steak or chop. It takes some flair to make eggplant fascinating.

When I spent time at the Pritikin Longevity Center I attended cooking classes and learned to cook vegetables as well as animal products with no added fats or salt. You'd be surprised how creative you can become.

When I read recipes I can usually figure out those that I can adapt by reducing the amount of fat, sugar, salt, etc. to make them acceptable for my needs. Of course, I also eliminate others that can't be changed without ruining the recipe.

There are many foods that can be helpful to you in reducing. You'll have to decide which of the ones I mention are for you, and substitute others of equal caloric value for those that don't appeal to you.

At this stage in your dieting career (since many of us have made it just that) you probably can judge calories fairly well. I don't have to tell you that corn-on-the-cob has fewer calories than creamed corn.

Ideally, I'd like you to stop counting calories. Work with foods that you know in advance are not fattening. That way you don't have to spend your energy figuring how much roast pork and applesauce you can fit into 200 calories!

I find that with a food that is low in calories, I don't need to know how much of it I can eat. I just eat. It always works.

Remember my advice: *always* have available in your refrigerator a small bowl of carrot sticks and celery (or radishes, sliced cabbage, cucumber, etc.). They must be fresh and appetizing to the eye and instantly visible. That means you cover the dish lightly with plastic wrap (not aluminum foil, which would make it invisible).

In a day or two discard any shriveled up leftovers. Sure, this may cost a few cents, but most vegetables are much cheaper than most junk foods. You are making an investment in a new figure. You are worth it.

Americans spend billions of dollars a year trying to lose weight. This includes money spent on diet food, diet books and literature, and visits to health spas and weight-reducing salons.

If you consider all that money, tossing out old vegetables will seem a mere drop in the expense bucket.

Along with the veggies keep a similar dish with bite-size pieces of chicken. (Just in case you didn't already know this, remove the skin, even if you love it.)

When you come home hungry and hit the refrigerator, the first thing you should see are these two dishes. I'm not about to promise that you will always eat these "good" foods. But even if you turn to them fifty percent of the time, you are halfway there. You may surprise yourself and even learn to like and, yes, even prefer, these to more fattening snacks. Crunchy foods satisfy an essential urge to chew. It doesn't have to be pretzels (which, I confess, I love); carrots fill the need equally.

If you have the kind of job that allows it, take similar nibbles to work with you. These days no one will think you are weird for toting your own food around. On the contrary, in the world of jet set society, hardly anybody eats anything anymore.

People are sipping mineral waters instead of martinis at business lunches and the most chic people rarely, if ever, allow themselves the luxury of eating the bread that is placed next to them. The waiter puts the bread down, you smile, and he knows he'll be taking it away, untouched, later.

People who lunch frequently during the business week rarely have dessert. Take my word for it, we are headed for the non-lunch lunch. You carry your plastic bag or container of raw cauliflower and you'll be the envy of your peers who'll be having indigestion over greasy hamburgers.

If you are still not convinced that you can comfortably carry this off, just bear in mind that it's all in your style. If you act like you are supposed to be behaving in a certain way, no one ever questions you. They admire you. To repeat: It's all in your style. So have some flair when you whip out your baggie of goodies.

◆◆◆◆◆

Let's talk salt.

Everyone knows that we are often told to reduce salt intake on a diet. But do you know why? Salt causes your body to retain water (also known as edema). Even if you know that water isn't real weight, when you feel bloated, you feel bloated. If you feel fat, you probably feel depressed. And, if you feel depressed you may start overeating. So, even though you know that the first weight you lose when you start a new diet is water, it's still uplifting to know that something is coming off.

Some people swear that salt has absolutely no effect on their fluid retention, while others blow up. If possible, cut down on salt. If you can't live without corned beef, eat it. But trade it off against the salted peanuts.

In addition to salt, fats and sweets can also cause edema.

I stopped salting my food years ago. Not because of fluid retention but because I have slightly elevated blood pressure. Since I already described my family history in morbid detail, you'll recall that all of them had high blood pressure. I keep mine well-managed.

I've cut down on salt. If food is presalted, I don't add any. You'd be amazed at how many people salt their food automatically before they even taste it. Once you stop using salt you'll be surprised how salty foods taste even with a very small amount of it in the preparation.

Taste first before adding salt. If you think the food needs it, add it, sparingly. You may discover new food tastes that you were masking with salt.

◆◆◆◆◆

How about chewing gum? There are different opinions about chewing gum, and I agree with all of them. I'll explain. Some say chewing gum replaces the need to eat, if only temporarily. Others believe that chewing will start you salivating and will turn on your appetite. Both can be true.

Sometimes not having anything in your mouth will stall your urge to eat because your appetite button hasn't been switched on. But there are other moments when you just have to have it. When that happens find a brand of chewing gum that has few calories (lots of these are available) and one that keeps its flavor and softness.

You might think I'm carrying on a bit much about chewing gum. However, often these "little" things make a big difference between success and failure. If you chew gum that gets hard fast and loses its flavor quickly, you are going to dispose of it and start another piece. Only a few calories, but they do add up.

Do you save calories with sugar-free gum? A stick of Carefree gum contains 8 calories. A gum with sugar, like Juicy Fruit, contains 10 calories. Not a big saving! Thus with gum, sugarless or not, moderation, as the ancient Greeks said, is the best policy.

◆◆◆◆◆

While we're at it, let's talk about low calorie candies. There are some that contain three or four calories. With candy, I feel pretty much the same as with other pretend foods. One piece of candy isn't going to make you fat; many pieces do. And, with low calorie candy, if you don't watch your intake you may discover you have consumed as much or more than you might have if you had indulged in one piece of the real McCoy.

Is having one piece of candy going to turn you into the Candy Monster who devours everything in sight? If you *honestly* think you can manage to have only the one piece, eat it. You probably will find yourself more satisfied that way. And, that sense of satisfaction can propel you forward. As we well know, the feeling of deprivation does not make good diet sense.

If you recall, I used candy as a diet trick, eating a piece before meals. It worked for me. But since you promised to be realistic about losing weight, you'll have to be realistic about this too. If you think you cannot eat just one piece of candy, don't have any at all, not even the low calorie type. Maybe the calories won't be hurting you, but if sweetness turns on your hungries, whether it's low or high in calories, it is better to pass it by.

◆◆◆◆◆

Sugar. As dieters, we recognize the negative effect of sugar on our bodies. There are scientists who insist that sugar is not a food at all, and if it was to be introduced today as a new additive, the Food and Drug Administration would ban it as unfit for human consumption.

Sugar can be addictive. It puts your body chemistry into a sudden high, and then an equally sudden low which creates an irrational desire for more sugar. There is also increasing evidence that sugar may be a contributing factor in high blood pressure. An Associated Press story described the results of research at Louisiana State University involving monkeys. It was discovered that monkeys on a diet of high salt and sugar experienced a rise in blood pressure exceeding that of monkeys fed only a high salt diet.

This doesn't mean that humans will react exactly the way monkeys do, but the thrust of the evidence points accusingly at sugar.

You may grumble from time to time because you have to make decisions about eating or not eating certain foods at certain times. Why haven't I simply outlined a day-to-day plan for you to follow? Most other diet books do that. But you have tried those and once the diet is ended, your climb up the scales begins again. I have you selecting your own food instead of relying on formula diets, so that from the beginning you are in charge of your own behavior.

Let's examine this attitude of responsibility in another part of your life for a moment. Unless you are homebound because of illness, you probably select your own clothing when you go shopping. Sure, you may ask your spouse or friends for their opinion, but the final decision is yours. It probably wouldn't occur to you to hand over to someone else the job of choosing your wardrobe. It should make the same good sense to select your own foods.

When we began, we agreed that you were going to take charge of your life. If you continue to let Dr. Atkins or anyone else dictate what you eat, you'll never grow up. You don't need that crutch. You can be in control.

There's no better feeling for a person who has struggled for years with weight than the satisfaction of losing it and keeping it off.

We know that meat is high not only in calories, but in fat as well. Do you like fish? Then eat lots of it.

Most fish is so low in calories and fat that almost anything you do in preparing fish, with the exception of frying it, can't add up to the calories you consume in a big steak. And the fats found in fish like salmon and mackeral are good for you. Simply grilled or broiled fish without added fat is a fraction of that count.

There is another reason to learn how to judge calories without actually getting bogged down in counting them. People start hunting for calorie charts that give slightly better counts. If you search, you *can* find calorie charts where one food may be listed as having fewer calories than on another chart.

Who are you foolin'?

If you want to believe that because a bran muffin is listed in one chart as having 105 calories, every bran muffin has the same count, you're back to playing kiddy games with yourself.

Now that foods have to be labeled as to ingredients and portions, I'm often astonished to find out that one portion of a giant muffin that adds up to 105 calories may only be one-quarter of the whole muffin.

It's better to recognize that certain types of foods are basically higher in calories than others. If you have a question about a food, don't eat it. If you have to ask yourself what part of that bran muffin you are about to eat adds up to 105 calories, chances are you already know the answer.

Bagels have become a popular food. They are sold nationwide and can even be found in other countries. Most people have the impression that a bagel is low in calories. This can be true. However, some are so big they contain more calories than you would choose to consume. There is no conformity to manufacturing bagels, so some contain fat, sugar, as well as "extras" like cheese, raisins, peppers, etc. Be alert and aware.

When I get bagels that are large, I cut them into three or even four slices and eat them over the course of a day—or maybe even two days. They become a planned treat that I look forward to.

As I suggested, if you concentrate on foods that are "good" for you, you won't have to be busy counting calories. However, if you feel you just must have a sirloin steak, go ahead, but follow the firm rule about trading it off for something else.

If you are accustomed to having a baked potato with your steak, kill that reflex habit that has you adding butter and sour cream without thinking about it. No butter and sour cream!

For years I used to cut my baked potato in half and dig out the inside. I gave that to my daughter, Jenni. I devoured the delicious (and nutritious) crispy skin.

Sometimes I think I was a pioneer. Today many restaurants offer potato skins on their menus. Unfortunately, they are often fried, or topped with melted cheese or some other equally high-fat, high calorie topping. You might as well have a Big Mac.

Today I eat the entire potato and top it with salsa or mustard or steamed mushrooms or any leftover vegetables.
Delicious!

Incidentally, if you want the skins on baked potatoes to be crisp, don't wrap them in aluminum foil. Even if it looks pretty, it prevents the skin from crisping.

Let's talk about pasta. No food is forbidden if you handle it intelligently. For many years I swore off all pasta. I promised myself I would eat it only in Italy. (That can be darned effective. Especially if you travel only occasionally, and even less frequently to Italy!)

Now that I follow the Pritikin Program, I often indulge myself with a pasta dish. And when I have time, I make my own fat-free tomato sauce*

The problem with pasta, or any other foods that you are used to really chowing down, is that you have to know when it's stop time. I've said that I control food and not the other way 'round, but I'm also realistic. There are devious foods lurking everywhere that want to take the command position away from me. If any foods seem too challenging when you are trying to lose weight, don't add to your problems by choosing them.

One approach to losing weight that works for me is a rule I try to stick to: IF YOU DON'T KNOW WHAT'S IN IT, DON'T EAT IT!

Thus, if you eat pasta at a restaurant with "mystery" sauce, you can never be certain of the ingredients. If you make it at home you have control.

I shy away from Chinese food, which I adore, for much the same reason. Most Americans have been brain-washed into believing that if you eat Chinese food you will be "hungry again in an hour."

Whoever said that hasn't observed what most people order in a Chinese restaurant. Platter after platter is brought to the table offering not merely tempting veg-etable dishes, but succulent pork and duck and beef. Gone is the Chinese restaurant style of the 1930's, where Chinese food consisted of a little meat sprinkled on a pile of sometimes unidentifiable vegetables.

Chinese cuisine is considered one of the great cuisines of the world, and you can eat too much of it just as you can of any other food. And it frequently is high in fat and salt.

I stay away from Chinese food because often the recipes are so complex that I just don't know what ingre-dients go into its preparation. Using my motto as a guide, I don't know what's in it, so it's not part of my regular food program.

I don't feel that I'm punishing myself. When I do decide to have Chinese food, it's a genuine treat. And when I eat it, I enjoy it without any thought of what it's doing to my figure. I trade off the Chinese food that I have that day by cutting down the next day. Or, by cutting down on other foods that same day.

Unless you understand that you cannot eat the Chinese food *and* all the rest of the food you usually do, you'll stay fat forever. On the other hand, just as soon as you begin to balance your food, you're on the way towards becoming thin *and* learning to be flexible about food.

Am I convincing you that *you* supply all the magic necessary to get thin? Believe me, your magic is greater than the promises and schemes of "experts" who haven't been through the struggle themselves. I've not only been there, but I've managed to win. I stay thin. I feel good. I look good. And I eat all the kinds of foods that I thoroughly enjoy.

Isn't mine a lovely situation to be in?

There's room for you right beside me. You can do it too. You can experience how great it feels to have people look at you with the same envy that you used to have for thinnies. You'll appreciate and enjoy it as I do.

Never for one minute do I take my thinness for granted. Every day I wake up pleased with the job I've accomplished. I want you to share this terrific feeling.

Before I had full confidence in my ability to live without certain foods, I used to buy "diet " things. One such item was "diet" jam or jelly, made with low-calorie sweetener. This is much like the cheesecake I mentioned before. Yucch. It does not taste like "real" jelly or jam. The useful purpose it may serve is to turn you off using jams altogether.

Happily, today there are many of varieties of "all-fruit" spreads which use only fruit and are sweetened with juices. And sometimes they aren't sweetened at all; the fruit is sweet enough without adding anything. Jams and jellies aren't so awful; they do contain sugar, the portion you eat is usually small enough not to worry about.

You usually don't *have* to use the substitute for the real thing. We always assume that certain foods are "fattening" and so reach for the lo-cal variety. Now that many foods are being labeled so that you can know their precise ingredients and caloric content, you'll find there are foods you can have in your diet that you used to exclude.

You will save money (since the lo-cal versions are invariable more expensive), enjoy the taste of real food, and still continue to reduce.

If bread is important to you, it's not difficult to cut in half the amount of bread you usually eat. Use one slice instead of two. They do this in Scandinavia and call it smorrebrod. You can, if you wish, put the same total contents on one-half the portion of bread.

Or, try eating the Asian way. Make a sandwich by using a leaf of iceberg lettuce filled with a bit of meat, chicken, or other fillings. Roll it up and eat it out of your hand.

Should you be skeptical, let me assure you that these are tricks that people use, *and they work.* Consider anything that may work for you. Don't worry about looking foolish. Keep your get-thin goal clearly in sight.

Each time you set a plate of food before you, decide in your mind to leave something on it. Even a carrot. It's a symbol of self-discipline to not consume everything in sight.

We've talked about the myth called "willpower." There is another, more persistent instinct. You can use it to full advantage. I call it "want power." You want one thing more than you want another. In this instance you want to be thin more than you want to stay fat.

Once you've got a bellyful of "want power" your problem is licked. Remember this each time you are in a temptation situation. Eventually, it will become part of you.

Carole's Simple Tomato Pasta Sauce:

In a large saucepan sprayed with food release (Pam, etc.), sauté two chopped garlic cloves. As this cooks, add chopped sweet onions to the pan and cook over medium-low heat. (If you like onions, use two large ones.) Cover the pan so they cook but don't burn. When soft, sprinkle about 1/8 tsp. of hot red pepper flakes over the onion-garlic mix. Stir. Add to this chopped, peeled fresh ripe tomatoes or, if out of season, two large cans of chopped tomatoes or thick tomato puree. You can find low sodium or no-added-salt varieties. Use enough to fill the pot almost to the top. It'll cook down. Bring to a simmer. Add fresh basil or dry, oregano, parsley and any other fresh herbs you like. Cook this uncovered as it reduces and thickens. Taste and adjust seasonings. After about an hour it should be finished. Use this on top of your pasta. It'll make a light, delicious sauce. Freeze unused sauce in small containers. Enjoy!

INTERMISSION

Five Rules to Liven Up Your Lightening Up

1. Eat small portions of many foods.
2. Keep refrigerated snacks of fresh vegetables.
3. Better a small portion of "real" food than an abundance of artificial "diet" food.
4. Give gifts of the things you love to eat to other people. Treat them to restaurant desserts, and feel proud of yourself as you enjoy watching them eat it.
5. Pick one food that makes you fat and avoid it for seven days. Vary this from week-to-week.

26

Change is the Magic Word

Change. That's what it's all about, isn't it? Trade off. Awareness. Choices.

SUCCESS IS YOURS FOR THE TAKING
IF YOU TRULY WANT IT

I have been telling you in plain talk that the answers are within you. It seems easier to believe that outside influences make you fat. That way you can wrap yourself up in your overweight, throw up your hands in frustration and feel sorry for yourself.

When you believe others make you fat you are easy prey for the next crazy diet to come along. So if that's the attitude you are comfortable with, put this book aside until you are ready for change.

Ah, but you have come this far with me, so I must be getting through to you. Stay with me, and you will end up like me—thin.

Have you matured enough to accept reality? Are you now ready to admit that you simply cannot lose weight by eating jelly beans for one week and expect to keep it off?

Are you ready to change your eating attitudes?

Now you know you needn't panic because you think you won't ever bite into a hero sandwich again. Now you know that you'll be able to eat anything you want.

I am a thin person. I eat fantastically well. And I'm not

talking about boring, "diet" food. By now you know there is no food that is forbidden: you can eat anything if you know how to handle it.

Isn't it more than just a little fascinating that "dieting" has come to mean going without food? Diet isn't a bad word; it's a word whose definitions we tend to forget. We forget that one definition is simply "a manner of living as regards food." Nothing there about fat or thin, either. (But you know and I know that if we are thin our physical condition is improved.)

It's not crazy to have you ask yourself again at this point, "Do I *really* want to be thin?"

If the answer is "Yes"—then what are you waiting for?

Think about the question. To get thin and stay that way you must make an agreement with yourself that you are willing to live with.

Are you ready?

Before reading this book, you might have been concerned about having to give up foods you love. I belong to gourmet groups where I dine on sumptuous wines and exotic foods. I'm thinner now than I ever dreamed I could be, and yet I once worried about giving up my security blanket foods.

You will be making decisions about what you are going to eat. *You* may choose foods that appeal most to *you*.

You've learned about tradeoffs. We trade things off against other things every day of our lives.

If you want to go to a film tomorrow night, you don't need me to tell you that you can't attend the ballet at the same time. Translate this to food.

When I was a child, a secret pleasure was one shared with my good friend, Anne. Once in a while we played hooky from school and went to Anne's house, because her mother worked. We had a ritual that never varied.

She always had My-T-Fine chocolate pudding and we ate it, hot. Right from the pot. We devoured it with no worry about weight or pimples, both of which appeared on our bodies quickly enough.

I think fondly of those days and the My-T-Fine chocolate pudding. If I want chocolate pudding today, I'll have it. If I want to eat the whole portion right out of the pot, I'll do that, too. And if I choose to, I'll enjoy it and not feel guilty about it.

BUT—of course there is a "but"—if I choose to eat the chocolate pudding, I am fully willing to trade it off against other foods I might be eating. I cannot have the chocolate pudding *and* my chocolate chip cookie and tea in the evening. I cannot have it *and* eat a sirloin steak and baked potato for dinner. I cannot have that pudding *and* still eat my bran muffin and jam in the morning.

Do I feel deprived? Not at all. Because *if* I want the pudding, I decide I want it more than the other foods. Sometimes I feel it's worth it. Other times I decide it isn't.

I'm dwelling on this because once you accept and embrace it emotionally, your eating life will become a rational one and having been needlessly overweight will come to seem tragic-silly to you .

The most effective change is for you to create your own individual eating plan, structured for your needs.

Since we have explored the positives and negatives of many popular diets, let's explore in depth just how a trained behavior modification expert works. There's some variation, of course, but if a one-to-one relationship is for you, this is pretty much what you can expect.

My friend Michael had tried everything. I mean *everything:* Atkins, shots in the backside, liquid protein, pills to curb your appetite, pills that promised to change your metabolism within three weeks. Invariably he lost weight. And invariably he always put it right back on.

He was desperate. Every magic or crash diet had failed. He'd spent thousands of dollars trying to stay thin and it never worked.

He had the problems universal among heavy people. For one thing, although he had been considerably obese for more than twenty years, he never forgot that he had once been a thin boy. He was convinced that any day that thin boy would emerge from his fat body. Fat was only a temporary state for him.

This attitude is not detrimental in itself. As a matter of fact, it is an asset. It's positive thinking.

On the other hand, he found it difficult to admit he had a severe problem about dieting. He could point to all the times he had lost weight as proof that it wasn't so.

He had a tremendous ego. It takes superhuman courage for a person who is capable in all other aspects of his life to confess that he has a problem that is out of his control.

How many people do you know (maybe even yourself) who keep saying, "Any time I want to, I'll get thin." "Nobody has to help me." "I can do it." Even when he tried Weight Watchers he was convinced that he was different from all those fat people.

What is it about being fat that is such an emotional issue? If your car has a flat tire, you don't think it's a personal weakness to have somebody else change it. On the contrary, you're relieved. Admitting you need help to lose weight needn't be any different.

It's no different than alcoholism or drug addiction. Overeating is *your* form of alcoholism, and the first step to the control of alcoholism is admitting you need help.

Admitting he had a problem that he couldn't solve himself was the big step for my friend. Once he admitted to the problem, the next step was realizing that he was the one preventing a return to his image of the thin boy.

Reality hurt his feelings, but he finally, reluctantly, admitted that being fat was his own doing. He doubted that anyone could help him get thin; however, he agreed to try.

And he sought the advice of a nutrition consultant, someone trained in behavior modification.

That was the second step. First he admitted he had a problem, and then he was willing to consider that he needed outside help. Personal diet counseling is particularly effective for people like my friend Michael because it is tailor-made for people who respond best to individualized attention.

What is an expert in behavior modification?

A behavior modification counselor is a person who may be trained in nutrition, who may or may not be a physician; but she or he is there for you and for you alone. If you question their sincerity, believe that there are easier ways to earn a living than trying to help frustrated overweight people reduce.

The approach stresses eating awareness. It isn't necessary to dig deep into your past to find out why you eat; your present eating patterns are more important. Otherwise, you can spend many months rationalizing about how you were forced to eat as an infant, or forced not to eat, etc., instead of using that time and energy to get thin.

The task is to help you develop certain eating patterns while breaking others, without feeling deprived. You find yourself getting in touch not only with your food needs, but with yourself.

Since no two people are alike, no two programs will be. Through their guidance and your own analysis you will discover those foods that turn on allergic reactions in your body, or which may trigger uncontrolled eating. Obviously, they should be avoided.

A behavior modification counselor is not going to be judgmental. You can change your behavior without a counselor to help. I did it. But if I was losing weight today I'd certainly welcome having a supportive and knowledgeable person backing me up.

Think of the times you desperately wanted someone to talk to who understood. Times when your spouse or best friend just wasn't there. Or worse, was the one who kept you fat!

However you go about modifying your eating behavior is up to you. the group approach of Weight watchers is supportive. So is Overeaters Anonymous which employs a sponsorship relationship where you have someone assigned to you. That person is a buddy who gets involved with your food problems.

If I hear someone out there saying they can't afford it, don't forget all the millions of dollars spent each year on diet-related foods. How many of *your* dollars are included in that amount?

Maybe the answer is you can't *not* afford it.

Whether you try a group approach, do it alone, or see a behavior modification expert, this is the time in your life when you have decided that you are never going to go on another fad diet.

I hope that you've made many promises to yourself in the course of reading this book. Have you promised yourself to be realistic about how much weight you feel you should lose? Are you ready to run your last and most successful race toward *permanent* thinness?

Then let's move up to the starting line.

INTERMISSION

The next time you find yourself eating out of control, remember that you can stop it. Promise yourself now that you will gain control. The moment you say to yourself, "It's over," is the moment that your binge will end.

27
How To Break a Binge

I'm not predicting you will binge. You may not. However, having been in your place, I know I sometimes do give in to impulsive self-destructive acts. Even now. If I expected perfect control from myself all the time, those moments I do fall would wipe me out. But remember, we are not always able to be totally in charge.

In the past, if you were average, you went on a diet and stayed on it for two or three or even four days, at which time you got tired or bored and you cheated. Then you felt guilty and discouraged, and you were off and running to recover the lost pounds. That's past. We're striking both "guilt" and "discouragement" from our diet vocabulary.

As a realistic dieter, learn to accept yourself as a person who sometimes will eat foods you would prefer not to eat; you occasionally will eat more food than you wish you had; and you will maybe have a binge or two, or three.

I do not mean you should plan to binge. You won't have to! However, if you are aware that it may happen, you will be better able to regain control of yourself and not lose too much ground. As a matter of fact, you may not lose any ground at all.

Here's how it may happen and how you might handle yourself. Your boss has told you he's passing you over this raise period. You come home expecting comfort from your wife and she's not there. There's a note telling you the twins need braces which will cost thousands of unexpected dollars, and she's taken them to the orthodontist. She adds the information that she may be late, so please feed the dog and yourself.

What's a man to do? It would be nice to think everyone can handle bad news by saying, "Golly, that's too bad, I'm going to sit down and have a few carrots."

The fact is you probably will start "soothing" your wounds by feeding yourself. Food, as we know, was the original pacifier, as it came from your mother's bosom, or from the bottle. Unfortunately, most people are only made more miserable when they binge. So we want to know how to stop it.

If you expect it to happen once in a while you will be able to abbreviate the duration of your binges. You will be able to look at yourself and say, "I'm doing it again!"

Whatever you do, *don't hate yourself!* Don't feel that this symptom of mortality means that you're "bad" or "a weakling."

The moment... *that* very instant ... is when you can turn it around. Awareness is suddenly yours. You know what you are doing. And because you have learned that all humans make mistakes, you *won't* hate yourself for failing. Instead, you will tell yourself, "I'm going to finish this mouthful and then I will put my fork down and walk out of the room."

Saying it out loud is even more effective.

It's no different than the promises you have been making not to eat at certain hours of the day. *A binge is controllable behavior.*

Any time you stop, it's over, and that's that.

What is most destructive about a binge is not merely the uncontrolled eating. It's also an excuse we have that once we binge, there's no point in continuing with our reducing program.

People who binge think the contest is lost. The effort has gone down the drain.

Nonsense! You didn't get fat overnight. So one binge—or even two or three binges—will not cause you to regain all the weight that you have lost. A binge is just an instance of being out of control. And now you know that you *can* get the control back.

Here's how I handle it.

The other night I had a wonderful dinner which was loaded with foods I don't normally eat. I ate and ate. I drank too. Lots of wine. Even as I ate I felt the waistband of my skirt tightening.

The next morning I couldn't decide whether I should or should not get on the scale. As I've described before, sometimes it helps and sometimes it definitely does not.

That morning, before I got on the scale I made up my mind that whatever the number, I'd make it work for me.

Sometimes I pick a figure that even I know can't be possible. After all, it's not really possible to have gained ten pounds no matter how much you've consumed. But just for that moment I pretend that when I step on the scale it will be ten pounds that I've added to my normal weight.

When I weighed myself and saw the needle move up three pounds that was within acceptable limits.

More often than not I would recommend not weighing yourself. Wait until the following morning, or even the day after that. My thinking in this case is, "What can the scale tell me that I don't already know?" You know you ate too much, so it may only depress you and cause you to continue eating. Best to wait until you know the news will be good.

What was my next step?

I went to my wardrobe and decided that it was important for me to be aware of how it felt carrying around those pounds. That meant I put on a very tight pair of pants, so I couldn't forget the effort it would take to close them. You probably have a pair of pants like that.

Sometimes I decide to wear something very loose fitting. I do that when I feel that wearing tight clothing is going to make me feel miserable and only cause me to feel sorry for myself and perhaps keep me bingeing. You learn quickly enough which path to follow. That's part of being honest with yourself.

At these moments my desire is to make myself aware that I need to retain control of my eating.

The next step is to plan that day's menu immediately. Make it a challenge—but one you know you will succeed with. Tell your spouse and friends that you would like their help that day because you want to get back on the reducing track.

Try to get involved in an activity that takes you away from food. Make a deliberate plan, and stick to it. If you like to use your hands, pick up your knitting. Or start sanding that old paint-stained table you've been meaning to. If your hands are busy working, they won't be available to feed your face. You'll feel pleased with yourself and that will have only positive effects.

Try to be with people. Being alone may encourage overeating. There's safety in numbers.

Whatever you do, don't wait until tomorrow. Because one day of control can probably undo most of the damage you think you've done.

It will also prepare you for other moments when you may binge again. It'll prepare you in the sense that you will have proved to yourself that you can get the control back. That way, when you recognize that "I'm doing it again" eating, you'll also be able to say, "I can take care of it."

Most of all, don't chastise yourself. Accept your behavior as that of a human with human frailties and step back onto the path you strayed from.

A binge is over the second you decide it is.

Your excess weight will continue to come off.

Bingeing frequently gives you a distorted sense of how much you actually have consumed. You feel blown up. But once you gain control you will give your body a chance to empty itself of that bloat. In a day or two, or three, when you get on that scale you may be delighted to discover that you haven't done *that* much damage.

28

The Pleasures of Being Thin

It's *great* being thin! I love it that people are astonished when I tell them that I used to be fat. I remember how I used to look enviously at thin people. Now I'm one of them!

Obesity is an illness that leaves no scar once you have recovered. Nobody can tell you used to be fat, unless you let them in on your secret.

Being thin helps to keep you thin. When you start getting positive feedback from your friends and from your mirror you will like what you see, and you'll want to keep yourself that way.

At this point you have learned many ways to get thin. You also know how to stay that way. Life can be pleasure-full when *you* take control.

I used to be a believer in luck, both good and bad. Then I started to observe that "good luck" seems to come to certain people again and again while "bad luck" tags along behind others with frequency.

I can't promise that being thin is going to change your luck. I can tell you that it changed mine. I feel so good about myself that pleasant things happen to me all the time. When you become thin and stay thin you'll realize you did it for yourself. You'll know you did it because you care about yourself. Don't be surprised if the quality of your life improves. The changes will reflect your much improved self-esteem.

You can do that, or you can play house with every new diet that comes along; lose some weight and then gain it back. That way you can continue to make your contribution to the hundreds of millions of dollars spent yearly by dieters.

A friend asked me what my gimmick was. What's the trick in getting thin? And more important, what's the trick in staying thin?

I asked him if he was listening carefully because I was about to let him in on the secret. As he bent forward so as not to miss a word I told him softly what he already knew. The secret is that there is no secret. The secret is that if you're fat, *you know what you have to do.*

However, I short-changed him. I gave him only half an answer. There is indeed a "secret" and it is so sound that you'll never find it in diet books, diet articles in newspapers and magazines or ads for diet products.

I shall share this secret with you shortly.

This book is for all of you who have gimmicked yourselves to the hilt. It's for those of you who have closets full of bran left over from the high-fiber approach to getting thin. It's for you, too, who have half-empty containers of liquid protein, crowded out by partially used tins of powdered protein.

This book is for all of you who have squirreled away diet pills from assorted prescriptions of those "emergency" times when you need help over that plateau period.

And let's not overlook those who have bowed to receive shots of HCG; or others who go in and out of spas and fat farms.

This book is for all of you who are ready to admit that no matter how many ways you have reduced, you have never managed to keep your weight off.

Most of all, this book is for those who want to devote their lives to the pleasures that eating can offer. If there is a gimmick in my way of staying thin it is in my determination not to eat any food that isn't going to give me pleasure. And, even more, to never miss those foods that do.

Most of those who stay fat believe they must satisfy their appetite too—but we are in control of when we eat. Yes, it involves adopting a mature attitude and sense of responsibility, which is nothing less than terrific.

I'm not fat and I don't miss any of my favorite foods. Ironically, I often eat more—even in quantity—than I did when I was fat. Planning when and what you are going to eat is the gimmick. It's exciting to have control over your food. You can stop thinking about dieting when you know in advance that you have a satisfying menu ahead of you.

When you are thin you'll get a genuine kick when people watch as you consume food with a hearty appetite and wonder "How does she (or he) do it and stay thin?"

Okay, Carole, you've told us all of that. But what is the ultimate way to get it off and keep it off?

You've waited a long time. There is a wonderfully sound way to lose weight.

Once while attending the International Book Fair in Frankfurt, Germany, a friend and I were having dinner. Roger Price, the humorist who created Droodles and Mad Libs, came along and sat with us. He watched intensely while I ate.

The next day he made his confession.

It seems he hadn't been particularly hungry and so didn't want to order any of the overpriced food. Looking at my slim figure, Roger assumed that I'd never finish the food on my plate. He'd eat my leftovers, and thus fill his stomach and save an easy twenty dollars.

You can imagine his surprise to see me consume everything, with obvious enjoyment.

When he told me the next afternoon how my appetite had foiled his plans, he asked, "How can you eat that much food and stay as thin as you are? You must be naturally thin!"

One comment like that makes it all worthwhile.

When it was announced to the book trade that I was writing this book, I found that I had indeed opened myself up in the way I knew would be necessary in order for me to be able to help others to lose weight.

Once you're thin, do you really want to tell people you were fat? You can see the eyes measuring you, trying to imagine how you looked some forty-five pounds heavier.

But if my success in staying thin inspires you, it's added pleasure for both of us!

Few of us want to be, but many of us are fat.

But *some* of us aren't anymore! Since you can't tell merely looking at people you never know how many people have successfully reduced. When I researched this book I asked thin people if they'd ever had a weight problem. I met a number of men and women who told me that they had been heavy. Without exception these were people who decided that they liked themselves thin and that it was worth the planning and trading off involved to stay that way. Not surprising (to me) is the fact that they were people who eat well and obviously enjoy food. If they can do it and I can do it you can do it too.

And now I'm going to give you the sure-fire way. It is so simple, so safe and sound that you're going to wonder why *you* never thought of it before!

29

Toward a Happy End— Beginning

A happy friend of mine who had been dreaming for more than twenty years about waking up thin made this amazing-to-him discovery. After two decades of wishing himself thin overnight, he now understands not only that it can't happen, but that if it did, the thinness would be temporary.

He had tried everything. He was a veteran of every kind of crash diet, starvation diet, foodless water fast, and pill swallowing, injection-enduring approach to discarding those extra pounds.

He knew that it no longer mattered whether the "blame" lay with his mother, his bad habits, or his sugar blues.

What did matter was that, logically, he had come to understand that the extra pounds were his own responsibility; that no one held a pistol to his head to make him eat food, and that there were certain truisms about "keeping it off" that none of the above dietary approaches contained.

His new found rule? "If it isn't natural, it won't endure."

In other words, any approach to weight loss that ends at some point will leave you as you were before. The only truly success-insured "diet" is one that you can live with for the rest of your life.

It sounds so simple, doesn't it?

He also learned the sad, scientifically-proven fact that weight lost rapidly will return rapidly.

His "new" approach to reducing was to *limit his weight loss* to a pound and a half a week.

He no longer weighs himself every day . He only allows himself to step on the scale once a week. That way he can compensate one day for the extra calories he may have eaten the previous evening.

He has chosen an extremely realistic approach towards reducing, *and it works beautifully!* He still has a great deal of weight to lose. However, he no longer is impatient because he isn't thin immediately. He loses his quota of a pound and a half each week—every week.

He has a goal chart that he fills in faithfully.

If he loses less than a pound and a half, he goes on a one-day semi-fast. If he loses more than a pound and a half in any week, he considers it a bonus, but he manages to not be unrealistic about his plan. He has accepted the responsibility for making himself heavy and now he accepts the responsibility for making himself thin.

What he is doing is so sound that sometimes he feels he has invented the wheel. He used to want to lose ten or fifteen pounds a week. And sometimes he did—and then put them all back on again.

But this pound-and-a-half is magic. He isn't putting his body into shock. He isn't depriving himself of food.

What he is doing is slowly but perceptibly changing the way he thinks and acts about food.

When he has reached his "goal" he won't have to make a drastic adjustment in his eating. He has gradually changed his eating habits. And these will be his habits forever.

After four months he had lost twenty-seven pounds. On crash diets he lost that in a month. *But this weight he is likely to keep off forever.*

He can congratulate himself as he succeeds. For the first time in years he's actually *enjoying* dieting. He has the pleasure of watching the pounds go off, gradually, but regularly.

This is the concept I want you to try: Weight loss slowly but intelligently, a day at a time, but measured by the week. If you fall into the pits, you have the opportunity to jump out immediately and recover before the week ends.

Believe me when I tell you that lasting weight loss is married to time. Radical changes in your eating habits or sudden large weight losses are temporary for they're almost impossible to sustain.

Plan for a year. Assure yourself that "Next year at this time I am going to be thin." Remember that woman I told you about who announced to her husband that she was going to enter college at the age of 50? When her husband tried to discourage her by saying that by the time she got her degree she would be 54 in four years anyway, and she said "So I may as well be 54 *with* a college degree."

Losing weight at this rate will also enable your body to accustom itself naturally to the slow but steady change. You don't need a crash diet to lose at this pace. As a matter of fact, at first you hardly have to "diet" at all. You can probably just pick a couple of foods to cut out or cut down, and, presto, four pounds gone that first month.

A psychiatrist I know insists that this gradual way is the only way she knows that people lost weight *and kept it off!*

I want you to try it. Embark on the gradual approach I have just described.

Don't fall into the trap of believing you must lose a massive number of pounds in a short period of time. You're not in a race. You're embracing a positive and effective way to change your weight even as you change your eating style.

Set your own goals, both in number of pounds to lose

and the length of time you'll take to lose them.

The time factor is not the critical ingredient. A pound a week? Why, that's fifty-two pounds a year—with almost no sacrifice and with its own built-in you've-taken-con-trol-of-your-eating-so-you'll-keep-it-off insurance!

What is important is that you get thin *and stay thin*. Naturally. Comfortably. And in your own way, eating the foods you like and liking the you that you're shaping.

Most psychiatrists, nutritionists and behavior modifi-cation specialists agree that this is the best of all possible methods.

Try it. It works wonderfully well. And one of these days you too can say, "I was once fat but I'll never be fat again!"

Good luck to you!